RICHARD S. GALLAGHER

DELIVERING
LEGENDARY
CUSTOMER
SERVICE

ISBN 1-59113-759-4

This publication is designed to provide accurate and authoritative information in regard to the subject matter covered. It is sold with the understanding that the publisher is not engaged in rendering legal, accounting or other professional service. If legal advice or other expert assistance is required, the services of a competent professional person should be sought.

> -from a declaration of principles jointly adopted by a committee of the American Bar Associates and a committee of publishers.

Original edition published July 2000 by Oasis Press,
ISBN 1-55571-520-6

Skills Development International
PO Box 4023, Ithaca, NY 14852-4023
sditrain@aol.com

Printed in the United States of America.

Distributed by Booklocker.com

– for my wife, Colleen –

Table
Of
Contents

Preface iii

Acknowledgments vii

Introduction: How to Deliver Legendary Customer Service 1

Section 1: Customer Skills 21

    Step 1: Communicate With Your Customers 23

    Step 2: Create a Quality Service Experience 61

    Step 3: Handle Difficult Situations With Class 93

Section II: Team Skills 117

    Step 4: Manage a Service-Driven Team 119

    Step 5: Learn How to Execute 161

    Step 6: Turn Your Whole Company Into the Customer
       Service Team 191

Section III: Personal Skills 211

    Step 7: Take Care of Your Most Important Customer 213

Summary: Delivering Legendary Customer Service in Your
  Business...247
Endnotes...261
About the Author...263

Preface

Companies today have mission statements, vision statements, and customer focus groups. Yet relatively few organizations consistently deliver a truly legendary service experience. These firms invariably dominate their markets, maintain higher profit margins, and are happier places to work. And they all have a secret behind their success, one that has surprisingly little to do with courtesy or "attitude." The secret is having a system behind their service.

The purpose of this book is to share the secrets of how to deliver legendary customer service in any business, using a step-by-step approach that you can put to work immediately to create your system. Excellent customer service has its roots in specific communications, interpersonal and leadership skills that have been proven to work time and again in real customer situations. If you use them properly, you will learn the secrets that drive many of the service leaders in today's marketplace.

When I was a young man, I became director of customer services for a startup software firm consisting of five people. We put these skills to work every day, and watched this company grow to become a major firm listed on the NASDAQ stock exchange. We survived and prospered in a hotly competitive technical field by providing a level of quality service that our competitors could not touch, and it was a magical experience. Moving from my own experiences into the real world, you will see a strong link between consistent, excellent service quality and success in the marketplace for businesses of any size. This book is designed to help you capture the skills behind the industry's best customer service, as a blueprint for your own success.

We begin with a look at the one-on-one relationship between you and your customers. There are basic skills that help you master the most common interpersonal transactions, such as active listening, communications skills, and how to create a bond of empathy and respect with people in any situation. We then explore how to create a consistent service experience, using factors such as what to say and how to react in common situations. Next, we develop a step-by-step plan for handling the most difficult types of people and situations, and teach you how to feel confident no matter what you encounter.

We also look at one of the most important issues in creating excellent customer service: your relationship with others inside the organization. People often misunderstand that poor service is often caused by poor teamwork rather than poor interpersonal skills, and we look at ways to help develop and maintain the important internal customer relationships that fuel your own service quality. We examine how to work together with others, manage your own team of service professionals, develop good metrics of service performance, and above all use customer service in a strategic sense as your organization's voice of the customer.

Finally, we look at the relationship you maintain with your most important customer: yourself. When you develop personal skills such as managing your time, your stress and the sense of balance you bring to this profession, you have learned one of the most important secrets of service quality that fires on all cylinders, every day.

This book is truly a survival guide. It is packed with tools for delivering excellent customer service in the real world – techniques that are not obvious to many people, which help you and your entire business become supremely confident in working with both the public and each other. They are drawn from years of experience, and the best practices of companies who truly provide legendary customer service. They really work.

Many people view excellent service as something that primarily benefits customers, or perhaps their company. In my mind, they have it backwards. Delivering legendary customer service benefits you and your own team most of all, which in turn benefits both your customers and the company. It fosters interpersonal and leadership skills that last a lifetime, and can supercharge your own career and personal growth. And when a whole organization learns to become service driven, the rewards can multiply far beyond personal benefits into a tangible impact on morale, market growth and the bottom line.

Above all, this book is designed to teach you that excellent customer service is not simply the domain of perky, happy people who never have a bad hair day, but the birthright of people like you and me. My wish for you, the reader, is to use the tools in this book to discover how fun – and profitable – the skills of legendary customer service can become in your own life.

RICHARD S. GALLAGHER

Acknowledgments

Teamwork is an important part of any good service experience, and this book is a product of the efforts of many others. In particular, I would like to thank the following people:

- People who generously provided information or background material for this book, including Louise Kirkbride of Acme Software, Lisa Mack and Donna Bizzell of The CBORD Group, Ellen Dudley, Dr. Milt Garrett of Garrett Resources, Mark Campagnolo of Joe's Restaurant, Dr. Martha Rogers of Marketing 1:1, Randall Pearson of The Pearson Group, Amy Hanna of Sheetz, Inc., Frank Gaines and the public relations staff at Southwest Airlines.

- Sidney and Raymond Solomon of The Solomon Press for being my literary agents, and for their know-how, editorial guidance and good humor in bringing this project to fruition.

- Emmett Ramey and his entire team of professionals at The Oasis Press, including editor C.C. Dickinson, layout director

Jan Olsson, copyeditor Janelle Davidson and cover artist Steven Burns, for a great job and a great working relationship.

- My wife Colleen for being my editorial advisor, sounding board and best friend for over a quarter-century and counting.

This project once began life in an earlier Oasis Press edition entitled *Smile Training Isn't Enough* (ISBN 1-55571-422-6). This new book adds a wealth of new content in areas such as specific communications and teamwork skills, as well as a core focus on bringing the best practices of successful service-driven organizations alive for people who work on the front lines of customer service every day. In closing, I'd like to welcome old friends and new readers alike, as we continue to explore the real secrets of truly delivering legendary customer service in your own environment.

Introduction:

How to Deliver Legendary Customer Service

I have always been fascinated by what makes great companies great. For example, two groups of people each start an airline, an overnight delivery company, a restaurant chain, or a small business. Both may succeed at first, but one company becomes a legendary firm that dominates its market, while the other one fades far into the background or disappears.

If you look closely at these companies, you'll often find similar products, similar market segments, and perhaps even similar mission statements. Very often, what differs is the service experience they deliver to their customers. In most industries, the industry-dominant firm is the often the one with the strongest service culture.

I am also fascinated by what makes great people great. If you look at who rises into leadership positions in your own business or community, here too you often see people with a strong service orientation. People who consistently deliver a quality service experience to both to their external customers and the "internal customers" they work with every day are frequently the ones who rise to the top of any organization.

This book is a step-by-step guide to what builds great organizations, and great people. It looks at the best practices of a service-driven organization, and breaks them down into steps you can put into practice every day. It unlocks the secrets between being "nice people" and delivering consistent, world-class customer service.

There is a System behind Great Service

When we think of leadership in customer service, we have a tendency to think of major corporations. And indeed, there is no lack of companies who have grown to dominate the world market on the wings of great service quality. For example:

The Ritz-Carlton hotel chain operates from a simple credo: "We are Ladies and Gentlemen, serving Ladies and Gentlemen." Its service culture is designed to anticipate and fulfill guest needs at a level that is unusual for even the hospitality industry: for example, if you frequently order certain kinds of snacks at one Ritz-Carlton hotel, you may find a refrigerator stocked with them on your next visit to another Ritz-Carlton halfway around the globe. Employees are trained to meet very detailed service standards ranging from eye contact to personally escorting guests when they ask directions, and are treated with equal respect as the most senior management. The results of this total service culture include both strong growth and industry recognition, including the Malcolm Baldridge National Quality Award in 1992.

Lands' End revolutionized the once-unusual idea of ordering clothing by telephone by providing a level of service and competence rarely found in most walk-in stores. Callers are greeted by staff who not only pride themselves on their "Midwestern friendliness," but can instantly access the measurements, care instructions and delivery time of their thousands of items, as well as a history of whatever you have ordered from them in the past. And their guarantee is absolute – they openly encourage the return of merchandise that is unsatisfactory, even if you have worn it for years.

Amazon.com is one company where you may never, ever speak with a human being. But excellent service quality has played a major factor in its growth to become one of the largest retailers on the Internet, where people can electronically browse and order from millions of books, CDs, videotapes, electronics, and other products. The Amazon.com shopping experience includes personal recommendations based on your past buying patterns, 24-hour on-line tracking of orders, responsive e-mail and telephone customer service, and the ability for customers and merchants alike to post reviews and information about their products.

There is no question that having a strong service culture is crucial to the growth and success of many of the world's market leaders. What may be less obvious is that world-class customer service can drive the success of nearly any business, or any person.

Here in my small hometown of Ithaca, NY, there was an Italian restaurant named Joe's. Originally a sleepy family restaurant that closed under the competitive pressures of the 1980s, it was re-opened several years later by a group including former chain restaurant executive and Ithaca native Mark Campagnolo. Their changes included extensive staff training using videos, tests and coaching, detailed service quality standards, a computerized system driving its kitchen operations, and a total dedication to a personal service experience.

When you visited Joe's Restaurant, it was not unusual for Joe's wait staff to remember who you are and what you ordered last time, or for a chef to offer to prepare a custom dish that you raved about on your last business trip to Chicago. Their attitude was perhaps best summed up by what one employee said when a customer asked him to find their waiter: "We're all your waiter. What can I do to help you?"

As a result of these changes, the difference between old Joe's and new Joe's – similar physical facilities both serving good Italian food – was striking. With almost no advertising or promotion, lines of people snaked out the door waiting to get into Joe's nearly every weekend. It eventually became rated among the top 300 private restaurants in the United States, and served as a case study for how business success can be fueled by consistent, excellent service quality.

People are often under the mistaken impression that good – or bad - customer service is basically a matter of courtesy. In reality, there is usually a system behind great service. It may start with courtesy and a positive attitude, but if you scratch the surface of companies who provide legendary customer service, you will find that it goes much deeper than that. Areas such as the skills people develop, how people are managed and motivated, and your company's guiding principles all help drive a consistent, successful service experience.

Conversely, most poor service has its roots in the lack of a system. Let's take a look at one case where bad service went far beyond a failure to be polite:

Years ago, one of my major consulting clients used a particular overnight delivery firm which was unique among the major delivery services - they had a chronic problem finding my house, whose street had been renamed a couple of years earlier. They would at times drive around for days with my "overnight" package before finally calling me, and the problem continued for months on end.

One week, a particularly urgent shipment was being sent to me. Knowing their past history, I called their toll-free "customer care center" and asked for the number of their regional office. They refused, saying that they did not give out that information. I then asked them to pass along detailed directions to my house to the regional office themselves. It never happened. Not only did the package not get shipped to my house, but they in fact called my client, mistook their street name for an identically-named city in Massachusetts, and shipped the package to their office in that city.

My problems with this firm even went beyond international boundaries. Once I taught a training program for this client in Montreal, and the client shipped me computers and training equipment together with a prepaid airbill to ship it all back to them. When it came time to leave, and I called this company's Montreal office to pick up the equipment, they refused to come because their own company's American account number was not valid in Canada.

Do situations like this affect their business fortunes? I'll never know for sure, but I do know that this particular company commands nowhere near the market share, or the mind share, of their larger competitors (all of whom, incidentally, know where I live). Moreover, problems like these won't be solved by teaching more customer courtesy courses. They stem from the lack of a system.

That's where this book comes in. If you critically examine how organizations and people succeed at providing legendary customer service, you will find that they can be boiled down into a series of clear guidelines. And the great news is that when you put these steps into practice, you and your own organization have the ability to create your own legendary service reputation, as a strategic competitive weapon.

These steps start with developing consistent interpersonal skills, and move on into how you manage your team, run your operations, and measure your performance. Finally, they touch on your own personal growth and skills. Taken together, they form a blueprint for how to create world-class service in your own environment – and why it requires much more than just trying to be nice people.

The Seven Steps

In any organization that provides legendary service, you will find several core areas where their people work differently from a typical organization. These areas encompass how they interact with their customers, the rest of their organization, and themselves. You can break these down into seven key steps.

Step 1: Communicate with Your Customers

The core of any service experience is the interaction between you and a customer. Companies who provide legendary service combine courtesy and a positive attitude with structured communications techniques that create a consistent strong rapport with people in any situation – in-person, by telephone, or on-line.

Step 2: Manage the Overall Service Experience

Beyond basic communications skills, certain core behaviors are part of a consistent service experience. Legendary service organizations have a keenly developed sense of "who we are" in working with the public that include guidelines for how to act, what to say and not say, and how to demonstrate service leadership on a daily basis.

Step 3: Handle Difficult Situations with Class

While the right communications and transaction skills can prevent most confrontations in the first place, knowing how to handle difficult people is an important professional tool for customer service. Top customer service professionals know how to defuse a crisis, and how to understand and manage common situations with difficult customers.

Step 4: Manage a Service-Driven Team

Few things have a greater influence on service quality than how it is managed. Customer service is a challenging profession that involves working with talented, creative men and women – and building a team relationship with your own management. Doing it well involves areas such as goal-setting, hiring, motivation, rewarding the right things, preventing burnout, working with peers, and coaching for high performance.

Step 5: Learn How to Execute

This is the single most important factor in making the leap from "nice people" to legendary service. Many customer service teams mean well but don't have their signals straight - for example, when people don't follow up on problems, don't know when they should escalate a problem to someone else, or don't coordinate well with other groups. Executing well involves setting strong operating standards for service quality, playing to your team's strengths, and measuring and tracking the right performance metrics. Above all, it means seeing each customer transaction through the eyes of your customers.

Step 6: Turn Your Whole Company into the Customer Service Team

To work effectively in a service-driven environment, you need the cooperation of an entire organization behind you. This means developing the important internal customer relationships that make your business a seamless whole to the customer, including clear lines of communication, a customer-driven chain of command, and a teamwork-based environment.

Step 7: Take Care of Your Most Important Customer

You cannot provide consistently good service unless you take care of your most important customer – yourself. These include personal skills such as time and stress management, turning your job into a profession, and keeping your career and life in balance.

When you put these seven steps to work in your own professional life, you create a real change in your service quality. They go far beyond mere courtesy, and into how to successfully manage the entire customer relationship. More importantly, they form a set of interpersonal and leadership skills that can drive your own personal growth, and last a lifetime. They are the core ingredients of legendary customer service.

On a global scale, the effects of quality customer service on the bottom line are dramatic. A study by the Strategic Planning Institute shows that companies who focus on customer satisfaction retain their customers 50 per cent longer, and spend 20 to 40 per cent less on marketing. Wharton professor David Larcker has found that in early 1994, stock prices of firms ranked in the top 25% of the American Customer Satisfaction Index (ACSI) rose at nearly double the rate of the S&P 500 over a six month period. And according to Bain and Company, a mere 5% increase in customer satisfaction levels can translate to as much as a staggering 85% increase in profitability.[1,2]

Putting quality service into action in your organization is a multi-faceted process with a simple core: maintaining a service focus in every aspect of your operations, whether they involve customer contact or not. Perhaps the most important aspect of these seven steps is that they interrelate with each other to create the environment your customers experience every day. This means that any of these areas can become a weak link in the service chain:

- When people don't know how to understand and manage difficult customer transactions, it becomes too easy to revert to human nature and say the wrong thing at the wrong time.
- If people in different departments cannot cooperate to solve a customer problem, no amount of courtesy will send a customer away happy.
- Without ongoing training and support, your employees may not have the know-how needed to serve people effectively.
- When people feel that they have dead-end jobs instead of careers, motivating them to go out of their way for people borders on the impossible.

Conversely, when all of these areas work together in harmony, the result is an environment that benefits everyone involved. Your customers will be happy and help evangelize your firm to others, your team will enjoy coming to work and being superstars, and your company will be profitable.

Putting the Seven Steps into Action

The best customer service experience that I ever had began one sunny afternoon at Dulles Airport near Washington, DC, on board a jet airliner with a flat tire.

My flight had just landed for a stopover at Dulles, on the way to Washington's National Airport, when we all heard a loud "thump" as we rolled down the runway. A flight attendant soon picked up her microphone and announced that a tire had blown out on landing. Because it would take at least another hour to change the tire and get on our way again, a tram would be sent out for those people who wished to get off the plane.

My party was waiting for me at National, and it would be only an hour's bus ride there, so I deplaned and got on the tram. Arriving at the gate, I walked the length of Dulles's massive terminal to the bus counter -- just in time to watch the last bus of the day for National Airport depart.

I went around the rest of the terminal trying to find ground transportation, with no success. Somewhat upset by now, I went to the airline's ticket counter and explained my plight. The ticket agent checked, and saw that my original flight was now repaired and about to depart. "But, it's out there on the airfield -- how will I get back on it?" I protested. She paused for a couple of seconds, then smiled and said, "I've got an idea -- follow me".

I was eventually led into the depths of the airport's baggage facility, where I waited while the ticket agent spoke to some people working there. A couple of them got on their walkie-talkies, and then the next thing I knew, I was being helped into the front seat of a baggage cart! The agent smiled and said, "We usually have better accommodations than this," and then waved goodbye as we roared full speed onto the airfield tarmac. A metal staircase was rolled up to the jet, and I walked back on board just in time for the ten minute flight to National.

While it was an unusual experience being personally escorted onto the airfield of a major airport, there is a lesson in this story that applies to almost any customer service situation. It is natural to feel that excellent service is, at its root, based on the relationship between you and your customers -- but cases like this demonstrate that there are often much broader issues involved when someone creates a great service experience. Knowing how to work as a team with the rest of their organization, and develop the acquired personal and team skills needed to support them, is what differentiates service superstars from people who are just marginally effective "nice people".

Many of these seven steps were at work during my experience at the airport. In that case, getting me back on that plane in Washington involved a lot more than one person's effort. If you look at the transaction closely, you will see a number of factors at work.

- About five other employees cooperating in a team effort, including a ramp supervisor, a baggage truck driver, and the flight attendants who let me back on board the aircraft. All of these people were able to drop what they were supposed to be doing and help me.

- People who were willing to cover for the ticket agent while she left her post.

- A management who valued satisfied customers over mere rule-following. When I returned home from that trip, you can be sure that I wrote a nice thank-you note to the airline on behalf of this agent. The response I got from the airline made it clear that this kind of behavior was encouraged, and rewarded.

- Above all, a ticket agent who was able to come up with a creative solution to a problem (essentially, turning me into a piece of luggage!), and then knew how to work within the rest of the organization to implement it.

In most cases, delivering consistent, excellent customer service is a skill that goes far beyond the individual customer transaction, and has its roots in how you relate to your peers, your employees, your management, and your own sense of professionalism. People who do this well know how to manage all of these aspects, as an integrated whole.

Good customer service is not an innate skill. It is all too easy for good-intentioned people to fail at providing quality service because it involves much more than being nice people or exhorting your staff to have a "good attitude." It is a set of best practices and learned habits that can become part of the corporate and personal style of any organization. Understand them, and you will discover not only a system for excellent service quality, but perhaps the most cost-effective means of improving your market share and bottom line.

Good Customer Service Is Really Much Easier

It is too easy to think that service quality is simply another product of the traditional work ethic, and that the most service-driven organizations today are populated by saintly people who do twice as much work as their competitors. Don't believe that for a minute.

If you compare what takes place in the transactions of a successful business versus a less successful one, you will discover an amazing fact. They generally aren't performing many more tasks, or necessarily spending more money. Invariably, however, their employees are enjoying their work more and their life seems much easier than places that don't please people as well. The vast numbers of people who send their customers away unhappy don't know what they are missing.

Perhaps what fools people is the difference between short term efforts and long term gains. A day's worth of transactions contain hundreds of opportunities where an extra few seconds here, a couple of minutes there, and a extra kind gesture at some point add up to a much different public impression. On a more global scale, the most service-oriented firms often work more efficiently than their competitors, as they invest in systems and procedures that are focused on the needs of their customers. In both cases, these efforts are seen as investments that pay off handsomely.

In my mind, one of the fundamental precepts of good customer service is that it is a great deal easier than poor service. Here are four reasons why.

Happy customers cost less money

The old saying "a stitch in time saves nine" is a good analogy to the economic impact of satisfying customers. It may seem to cost more in the short run to cheerfully replace defective products, take care of a special request, or turn a problem into a great service experience. But if you compare it apples-to-apples over the life cycle of a product or service, it is almost always less expensive to satisfy people sooner rather than later.

Take the case of a man who bought a used car from your dealership last month. He now comes into your service department with a funny noise in the dashboard, exactly two days after your 30-day warranty has expired.

It might save you 40 bucks or so right now to tell him, "Sorry, you're too late for a free repair". But when you look at this transaction over, say, a three year period, you may really lose much more than that. For the next two years that he owns the car, he could patronize a more cooperative dealership for repairs. When he buys his next car, it may be at another dealership. And the dozen or so friends he tells about the lousy attitude he experienced at your dealership might shop elsewhere as well. In a case like this, you could win the 40 dollar battle and lose the four thousand dollar war.

As you move to the real world, other cases are much less subtle than this. Poor service has been at the root of many a lawsuit, and many a job termination.

Perhaps the most important financial cost is the effect an overall reputation has on an organization's bottom line. A truism in marketing holds that a satisfied customer will talk to four people about your firm, while an unhappy one will talk to eleven people. And over time, an amazingly consistent common attitude begins to emerge within a market.

Happy customers require less time

Whether it's relatives or customers, it seems that the more fervently you wish that someone would go away, the less likely they are to do so.

Let's say that you are taking your demanding Aunt Edna, who complains about everything, out for dinner. The wait staff might well be tempted to ignore her, but that often turns out to be a near-fatal mistake, and your repast may soon turn into a test of wills as she demands every bit of service that she feels entitled to. On the other hand, if the waiter solicitously asks her what he can do to make this a great meal, and smiles attentively at her requests, she is much more likely to remark "what a nice young man," and then return to her liver and onions.

This same principle applies to all of your customer relationships, both inside and outside the organization. Customers who like dealing with you will do their best to cooperate with you, and teams who work together spend less effort than teams who don't. A consistent, proactive approach to good service is not only good policy, but a move that generally cost-justifies itself.

Happy customers come back

It is a rare business that doesn't need "repeat business" to survive. It is a truism in sales that making sales to existing customers takes less than 5 per cent of the effort needed to sell to a new customer. Whether it's restaurants with their "regulars", or your uncle who always bought Fords, the customers who are so happy that you can plan on them are the key to most successful businesses.

Many management experts now advocate going beyond customer satisfaction to what they call *customer delight*, where customers are so pleased with you that they do not want to look for a better deal. These are the kinds of customers who can go beyond repeat business, and become evangelists for your organization. The statistics behind this are sobering. A recent study by Xerox found that when customer satisfaction is ranked on a scale of 1 to 5, customers who give you a ranking of 4 are six times more likely to defect than ones who rated you a 5![3]

If your business depends on making a sale, one of the hardest aspects of your job is overcoming a person's buying resistance. When you build a business around "delighted customers" who go out of their way to deal with you, you have taken care of the tough part already.

Good customer service is more fun

While treating customers well makes your life on the job more fun, this may be putting the cart before the horse. It is probably more accurate to say that having fun at what you do leads to customers being treated well. Either way, a customer-oriented working environment is generally a much happier place to come to work to every day.

I once lived near Pittsburgh and I had a favorite restaurant for lunch. When I took my usual table there, I was always greeted with a broad smile and "Hello, hon! Coffee?". I wished my own relatives would stop by as often as these people did to offer me more gravy, coffee, or a piece of pie. I once even heard the bus boy mutter under his breath that he was the fastest bus boy in the business, and one week, the manager announced an employee's birthday over the intercom, to applause from the diners.

In short, everyone seemed to put that little extra bit of gusto into everything they did. And despite being on a block that was crowded with restaurants, they were so busy serving customers that it was often hard to even get in the door. There was never an empty table there at lunch. What I really noticed was the way that the staff would laugh, kid around, and help each other out. These people were having fun.

The Payoff for You and Your Team

These issues are all things that are better for your organization when it makes good service a priority. More importantly, there are clear benefits for yourself and your team in developing strong customer relations skills.

Job satisfaction

Treating customers well has positive side effects on your own state of mind on the job, and the experience of sending people away happy wherever possible is a powerful daily stimulant each and every work day.

Career advancement

Almost any successful person in a leadership position today can credit at least part of their success to learning good interpersonal skills, and applying them to their work setting. One of the best things about customer service as a profession is that it serves as an excellent training ground for almost anywhere a person wishes to go, be it the front lines or the boardroom.

Higher income

People who set a goal of being the best in a service environment inevitably find themselves better compensated, and with more promotional opportunities, than their peers.

Organizational growth

When you treat customers well, you make a tangible contribution to the success of your own organization, which in turn yields benefits to your own career prospects within it.

Self esteem

Strong interpersonal skills with the public are traits that add to your own self confidence in almost any life situation, on or off the job.

Above all, learning the art of providing excellent customer service makes your profession a much more fun place to spend half of your waking hours or more -- and, in a very real sense, helps make the world a better place for those around you.

As we explore the various aspects of practicing good customer service, we will see that doing this well is often simply a matter of developing new habits and new perspectives in managing your relationships with the people around you. In return, the payoff in your own life is often immediate, substantial, and long lasting.

Doing Well By Doing Good

The seven steps outlined in this book work together in harmony, with each being equally important to maintain your equilibrium in providing excellent customer service. This book will explore each of these areas, and along the way, look at many of the real day-to-day practicalities of working as a customer service professional.

When these values become integrated into the daily operations of your organization, excellent service can go beyond good business practice to become an individual passion for everyone on your team. As the manager of a customer support call center, my staff and I have picked up the phone every day to speak with people, often over a hundred per day, calling with problems or complaints. They were rarely happy when they called, but our surveys showed that the vast majority came away very satisfied, and we took great pride in how well we did it.

Whatever your company does, the end product of customer service is happy people. When it's done well, there's no profession quite like it. For me, few things in life are as satisfying as hearing someone's tone of voice change to appreciation, seeing a tough problem solved, or having a customer say that they were so pleased they would write to our president. To have it happen dozens of times a day is one of the happiest jobs in the world.

There is a difference between having a good attitude and developing professional customer service skills, and this book is intended to be a roadmap to acquiring both in your work with people. In a sense, the skills that we discuss in this book form a good training ground for any endeavor in life -- because, at many levels, we are all constantly serving people in our lives as customer relationships. As a result, learning how to create a good service experience for your customers in business is an opportunity to develop skills that can become an integral part of your own personal style and last a lifetime.

Section 1:

Customer Skills

Step 1:

Communicate With Your Customers

Customer service starts and ends with the relationship between you and the people you serve. It is here, on the front lines, where great customer service is ultimately delivered in the eyes of the people who purchase your products and services. This makes interpersonal communications skills a great place to start in your quest to deliver legendary customer service. One common denominator among truly world-class organizations is that they consistently communicate well with customers, and this chapter is designed to give you the same kinds of skills in your business.

Communicating well with customers is as much a science as it is an art, and here we will discuss specific techniques that you can put to work immediately to improve your service quality.

They go far beyond the human nature of simply trying to be pleasant, into detailed steps that you can learn and practice in situations such as face-to-face, telephone and on-line customer transactions. Use them consistently, and you will gain both happy customers and a deep self-confidence in your own ability to handle typical customer situations. More importantly, excellent service will become not just a skill, but a habit.

The Myth of "Attitude"

One of the greatest myths about customer service is that it revolves around having a good attitude. The perception that customer service is basically a matter of being "nice" is true only to the same extent that baseball is simply a matter of swinging a bat and catching a ball. In actuality, professional baseball players develop a number of more subtle skills, such as reading signs, laying down bunts, and studying opposing pitchers, to put on a show that looks almost effortless to us as fans. In the same sense, professional customer service experts also perfect certain basic communications skills designed for interpersonal transactions. These skills are teachable and combine with what we presume is your already-good attitude to handle these transactions effectively.

Here is one experience I had dealing with a customer service representative with a so-called good attitude.

I had been involved in a minor auto accident, and needed to rent a car while mine was being fixed. A perky, friendly, articulate young woman helped me fill out the paperwork, and escorted me to the rental car with a smile and a wave. The next day, as I was walking out to the car from work, a co-worker pointed out a long dent across the underside of the door. Needless to say, I was very upset about this, since being involved in two accidents within two days doesn't go over very well with your insurance company.

I went back to the rental agency, and Miss Perky was all smiles as she told me that she was "very, very sorry, Mr. Gallagher," but that I was responsible for any damage to the car. I explained that I had not hit anything with it at all, and couldn't understand why there was a dent in it. It was to no avail, other than another congenial round of "I'm so sorry, Mr. Gallagher". At that moment, another man walked by behind the counter. I asked him about this problem, and he quietly said, "Let me check into this." A couple of minutes later, he came back and said that the car had indeed been damaged by a previous renter, and that I wasn't at fault.

If these employees had taken a course on personality skills for customers, Miss Perky would have been at the top of the class, and Mr. Quiet would have been comfortably in the middle somewhere. But I received a much better service experience from him than from her. While some things that one might call attitude are, in fact, very important in dealing with customers -- like caring about people, being responsive, and being polite -- there is a much broader range of skills involved in most successful customer transactions.

If you were to observe a large number of customer transactions yourself, they might appear at first glance to vary as much as patients in different rooms of a hospital. On closer inspection, however, most customer interactions fall into predictable patterns that require certain talents to bring to a successful close. You could summarize these skills as falling within one of four core areas:

- Communication
- Action
- Respect
- Empathy

You can think of this approach by its first letters: C.A.R.E. To distill its most important aspects into one single sentence, it would probably read something like this: A good service experience is the result of how well you interact with people, *what* you do and *how* you do it being equally important.

Following is a detailed look at each of these areas and see how they affect the way that you and your customers relate to each other.

Communication

Communication is a matter of listening and talking. At another level, it also shows in areas such as your body language and tone of voice. Most importantly, is has its roots in how well you can transfer both information and feelings between yourself and another person.

Many people view listening as the absence of speaking. More correctly, it is a very active process that conveys acknowledgement about what the other person is saying. Similarly, when it's your turn to communicate, doing it well involves much more than just talking. It ideally clarifies the other person's thoughts and then responds with information from you.

If you've ever had the vague feeling of annoyance yourself in dealing with a customer service person, and couldn't quite put your finger on why, the chances are good that you experienced a case of someone hearing and speaking but not communicating. If we stop and analyze the elements of a conversation to look dispassionately at what is -- or isn't -- accomplished by the words being said, we'll find some key differences between successful and unsuccessful transactions. As an example, let's take the case of a less-than-ideal conversation between a real estate agent and his client, examine it in detail, and then try it again with better communications techniques.

Customer: My house hasn't sold in the last six months.
Agent: The market's slow.
Customer: I'm losing over $1000 a month! What should we do?
Agent: I don't know what to tell you.
Customer: Well, what if we rented the property?
Agent: You could.
Customer: Or how about us lowering the price?
Agent: That wouldn't hurt.

There are several problems in the dynamics of this conversation:

- The customer is not getting acknowledgment of his feelings or even the specifics of his situation.
- The customer wants information about why his house might not be selling and is not getting it.
- All of the ideas for a solution are coming from the customer, while the real estate agent, who is theoretically being paid to help the customer, is passive.
- Little feedback is being given to the customer's ideas. Each of them might be a great idea, or a lousy idea, depending on the

circumstances. For example, if the market is so poor that even a substantial price reduction would not sell the house, the customer might be ill-advised to cut the price. Conversely, a decision to rent may cost more in the long run than a small drop in price or the addition of a fresh planter of flowers on the front porch. But the customer is not getting this kind of information.

This example gets to the essence of active listening and speaking. Done well, it should involve acknowledgement, feedback, sharing of information and a sense of closure. Look at the same transaction again, handled differently.

Customer: My house hasn't sold in the last six months.

Agent: I know how frustrating that is. You should understand that the market is somewhat slow right now: your house is priced at $85,000, and the average sale I'm seeing on homes like yours is coming through at more like $81,000. Also, the average time on the market is up to about 120 days.

Customer: I'm losing over $1000 a month! What should we do?

Agent: That is a lot of money to be losing. Let's look at our options: you could cut the price, offer better terms such as owner financing or down payment assistance, or perhaps rent the property until the market improves.

Customer: Well, at least I know what we are up against. Let's cut the price by another $5000, and give this another couple of months. If that doesn't work, we'll probably rent out the house.

Agent: That sounds fair to me. I'll list your new price this afternoon. I hope that we can sell it soon.

In this case, the customer will probably be much more likely to leave the transaction satisfied, and feeling like the real estate agent is a partner in solving his problem. Here are some of the specific things that the agent did right in this discussion:

- He acknowledged each of the customer's concerns directly, both about the lack of a sale, and the amount of money the customer was losing.

- He demonstrates interest in the problem by sharing information about its causes.

- He proactively offers solutions to the problem, and enough information about these solutions to help the customer make a good decision.

- He allows the customer to decide what is best for him.

- When a course of action is proposed, he gives the transaction a sense of closure by agreeing to the action item of changing the price, and then reaffirming his concern for the customer's agenda.

There is also an equally important non-verbal aspect to these communications that doesn't come through on paper. Body language such as good eye contact, smiling, a firm handshake, and a relaxed, open posture help set the tone for whatever is being said. Similarly, controlling your tone of voice is important to communicating what you choose to say, rather than letting your surface emotions dictate its content. In both cases, these are skills that improve with practice. The atmosphere that a professional customer service specialist creates could be likened to an athlete who puts on his or her "game face" before a contest. In my own career managing a software help desk, for example, we made it a point to give customers with difficult problems a particularly warm welcome, and make it clear that we knew what we were doing in trying to solve them.

Some basic rules for good communication with customers are:

- Welcome customers with your greeting, tone of voice, and body language.
- Listen actively by paraphrasing and acknowledging the customer's statements.
- Use action-oriented words and phrases.
- Provide information in response to the customer's concerns, and proactively suggest related information that may be of interest.
- Close the transaction by summarizing the action items and obtaining the customer's agreement to these items.

If you analyze transactions which satisfied you as a customer, you will probably observe a great deal of active communication going on -- both speaking and listening. Done well, it represents one of the single most important aspects of dealing with customers.

Action

Sending a customer away happy from a transaction can be only half the battle. Have you ever had the experience of ordering something from a cheerful, articulate person, and then having it never show up? Or calling repeatedly about something, being told that "we'll take care of it", and having it never happen? Ironically, communicating well with people can be an opportunity to create a very poor impression on people, if there is no follow-through on what needs to be done. Taking action, both during and after the transaction, are just as important as what you say to people. Enthusiastic, action-oriented words to customers represent an important way to make them feel good, but the proof of the pudding is in taking action to close the transaction.

There are a number of ways to show a willingness to take action with customers.

Provide closure

Before ending the transaction, provide a sense of closure by summarizing what action items remain and provide the customer with information such as:

- What will be done
- What the customer should try
- When to expect a call
- When the product will be delivered

or whatever else is appropriate to the situation.

Deliver what you promise

Promise what you can deliver, deliver what you promise, and resist at all costs the temptation to make things seem better than they are. Faced with a customer who might complain, or push for a better deal or not buy what you are selling, some people fall into the trap of becoming euphemistic about the situation. They may tell customers that "we should finish your project soon", or "the check is in the mail", to avoid the consequences of giving customers a more accurate appraisal. It is far easier in the long run to learn how to comport yourself assertively than it is to pay the price for misunderstandings with your customers.

Let's take a look at the difference between being "fuzzy" and being proactive in sharing both the good and bad points of a transaction with the customer. Too often, an encounter will go like this:

Customer: When can you install my tires?
Service: Oh, probably soon.
Customer: How soon?
Service: We'll give you a call as soon as they are done.

(two hours later)

Customer: My tires aren't done yet?
Service: Well, we're pretty backed up today. One mechanic is out.
Customer: Why didn't you tell me this earlier? You said that these would be done soon! Now, I don't want these tires after all. Let me speak to your manager...

At this point, whether deserved or not, this customer perceives a lack of honesty in the company's relationship with her. She correctly feels that she should have been entitled to be given enough information to fairly negotiate the action items of this transaction, namely, whether to buy their tires and when they could be installed. As a result, even if she eventually becomes resigned to purchasing these particular tires, she may never patronize their company again. Here is a much more professional approach to the situation:

Customer: When can you install my tires?
Service: We'll be glad to get these done as soon as we can. However, we must tell you that we are pretty backed up today, and one mechanic is out. If you would like, we could have this done by the end of the day, and we do

have a courtesy van if you need to go somewhere. We can also get this scheduled for anytime tomorrow.
Customer: Well, in that case, Monday might be better for me.
Service: That would be fine. Would morning or afternoon be better for you?
Customer: Early afternoon.
Service: How about 2 PM on Monday?
Customer: That would be fine. Thank you very much.

Some (mercifully few) people who sell for a living may take exception to this scenario, thinking to themselves, "How about the case where you tell the customer that it will take all day, and because of that, they run off and buy someone else's tires?" Of course such situations can and do occur. Nevertheless, honesty is still always the best policy. If your product or service has enough advantages to overcome negatives such as scheduling problems, then the customer will still want to do business with you. Moreover, if schedule is an important factor in the customer's decision process, they have a right to base that decision on accurate information.

This often becomes an issue of short-term versus long-term objectives. In this case, it is putting a single sale ahead of the customer's desire to do repeat business with you. Remember the truism in customer service that when people are happy with a product or service, they will tell four people about it, and if they are not happy, they'll tell eleven people. Frank, clear information about action items is one of the best ways to send people away being happy with your service, in almost any situation.

Take care of commitments

Above all, have a system in place that ensures that commitments can be taken care of. Whether this system consists of a sacrosanct corner of your desk where today's follow-up items go, or a corporate on-line database which connects service requests to the appropriate parties, such a system should prevent action items from getting lost in the shuffle of your daily work.

Perhaps the key issue in taking charge of the action items in a customer service transaction is to be proactive rather than reactive. Let it be you, rather than the customer, who summarizes what needs to be done and sees it through to completion. Here again, a little extra attention and a very small expenditure of time will yield dividends in both customer satisfaction and preventing the need for customer follow-up.

Respect

Everyone craves respect, and it is usually easy to respect people who are nice to you. The problem is, many customers will not have their best foot forward in dealing with you. This is part of the nature of customer service, because people often bring you problems or needs which frustrate them. To service these people effectively -- and to make the process smoother and quicker for both parties -- it is important to convey respect for the people you deal with, and preserve their dignity even when they are unhappy.

Doing this well may involve adjusting your job perceptions, from one of "getting rid of customers" to making them feeling as good as possible. The great paradox here is that when you make people feel welcome to deal with you, they will bother you less: the long way around is the shortest way home. Their impression of you and your organization may depend more on the amount of respect that they felt than the actual solution to their problem.

Also remember, in the heat of the transaction, that it can be a small world.

I'll never forget one summer in college, when I was a short order cook at a faculty and staff club at the university. I grilled hamburgers, prepared sandwiches and served customers with aplomb – with one exception. One day, my hand slipped as I was handing a bowl of soup to a well-dressed woman, and oops ... soup du jour all over her arm. I apologized profusely. She glowered and walked off. Years later, starting my first regular full-time job as a customer service technician at that school's computer center, my face must have reddened a bit as I was ushered into the office of my new supervisor: Ms. Soup-du-Jour. In my case, I was fortunate: we became close friends and colleagues over the years, and she claims not to even remember the soup incident. But it did serve to remind me that there is no such thing as an unimportant transaction.

Some tangible ways to practice showing respect for your customers, beyond practicing good communications and problem-solving skills, are listed here.

Use the customer's name frequently, where possible

Whenever appropriate, use the customer's name. This technique works well as a consequence of the times we live in. most customer transactions are still handled very impersonally, and the use of someone's name stands out as a mark of attention and respect.

There is an interesting bit of history behind this phenomenon: in times long past, titles such as "Sir" or "Madam" were used as a sign of deference, and it was considered a social faux pas to address a customer bluntly by name. Today, this convention has become so ingrained in standard customer service lingo that it now often has the opposite effect. Compare the phrases, "Sir, your car isn't ready yet" and "John, your car isn't ready yet" and you will see what I mean.

Acknowledge the customer's feelings

This is not the same as agreeing with these feelings: when a customer makes an unreasonable request, for example, the best policy is to acknowledge that this is important to them, and then proceed to outline more reasonable alternatives. Let's look at an example:

> **Customer:** This word-processing software doesn't handle tables or graphs! I can't complete my project because of this. How can I fix this problem?
> **Support:** It sounds like you need this for your work. I'm sorry that our software doesn't support this. I'm afraid that it's not a capability that we plan to have in the near future.
> **Customer:** But your advertisements say that this is a full-featured word processor! Isn't there a way you can fix this?
> **Support:** I'm sorry that our software doesn't handle this. I can, however, authorize a full refund if you would prefer to return the software.
> **Customer:** Hmmm ... I guess that would be fine.
> **Support:** I'll be happy to take care of that for you. Send the disks to my attention, at the address on the box, and we will have a refund to you within the next week.

In this case, the customer is frustrated and wants to get back to work right away, but this is not possible because of a basic limitation of the software. In response, the support specialist acknowledges the customer's concerns, states clearly what is possible (a refund), what is not possible (an immediate fix to the problem), apologizes, and then services the customer's decision to obtain a refund.

Separate your feelings from the job at hand

Particularly when a customer is agitated or hostile, work hard to separate your personal feelings from the needs of the transaction. This is a skill that takes time and practice to perform well, and it is important to bear in mind that while nobody is perfect, neither is anyone totally bad.

I personally use a technique that I refer to as the "Uncle Bob" rule in situations like this.

In my case, "Bob" was an older customer who seemed to push all the wrong buttons with our staff. Arrogant and hostile, he regularly called with problems that were ultimately caused by his own ignorance. We prided ourselves on keeping our cool in the face of customer hostility, but Bob posed a special challenge. One day, I remembered a TV movie that I'd seen years ago. It concerned a man who was hostility personified in public, but who had a soft spot for his family. At home, he became a sweet, loving family figure that his clients would never recognize.

I still don't remember the name of that movie, but from that day on, whenever Bob would call, I would bring to mind an image of him as jovial Uncle Bob, about to go home to his family – and it worked. I found that I was treating him with an extra dose of kindness. The smile on my face and the calm tone in my voice were real, thanks to a mental image.

There is sound psychology in the "Uncle Bob" rule: according to many experts in the field of human behavior, our subconscious mind cannot differentiate between imagined experience and real experience. In fact, many of us already practice this every day in reverse; when people get on our nerves, we have a tendency to build them up in our minds as horrible, nasty people who are much worse than they could ever really be. We then take those mental images and act on them, with our manner, our tone of voice, and the amount of effort we put in. And all too often, we make our worst fantasies of people come true by acting as if they were really that way! Yet there is powerful good in positive mental imagery of your customers. The great American humorist Will Rogers summed it up best when he said, "I never met a man I didn't like." In his lifetime, he probably met the same kinds of people you and I do. But he was mentally determined to like them, and he succeeded in seeing the good in even the worst of them.

So this week, give Uncle Bob a try -- you'll be truly surprised at how much it helps! Sometimes this technique has its limits. One day, one of my staff came into my office after a particularly trying phone call and said, "I've decided that even this guy's nephews can't stand him!" But in general, treating people like they're wonderful helps people to be wonderful more often than you can imagine.

Empathy

Picture this: you see a doctor about something that is bothering you. The doctor gives you the proper information and prescribes the proper treatment but is cold, clinical, and indifferent to your feelings. Now, picture another doctor who listens intently, reassures you that your feelings are perfectly normal, and then prescribes the same treatment after asking how you would feel about it. Which doctor are you more likely to return to?

All of the other customer skills -- communication, action, and respect -- represent the basic, necessary ingredients to servicing a customer. Yet like the first doctor, you can do all of these things well and still do, at best, a minimally competent job unless you develop an empathy for the customer's situation, and convey that empathy to the customer.

Empathy is another one of those traits that would seem to be a matter of attitude, and indeed, true empathy springs best from a genuine concern for the customer and their problems. At the same time, techniques such as the following are effective ways to convey empathy during a transaction.

- Use "feeling phrases" to convey an understanding of the customer's problem, and express a desire to solve it. These feeling phrases go beyond the specifics of what you can or cannot do, and are intended to demonstrate your empathy with the customer's situation. Phrases like, "That sounds like a pain in the neck," "Boy, I'd be upset with that problem too," or "That must be slowing down your project -- let me see what we can do to help" help set the stage for a positive, productive transaction with the customer.
- Paraphrase -- rather than simply repeat -- what the customer tells you before you give your answer.

Here is an example of how you can convey empathy.

Customer: I'm having a hard time installing this CD-ROM drive.
Support: It sounds like you have a challenging installation on your hands. What can we do to help?

> **Customer:** When I try to use it, the computer gives me a "general protection fault" error message.
>
> **Support:** So, you have the hardware installed, and it fails when you access it. This is a very common problem, and I think we can get this resolved. Would you have time to go over a few diagnostic tests with me?
>
> **Customer:** That would be great.

As discussed earlier, restating the customer's concerns is an important means to check your mutual understanding of the situation. When you paraphrase what the customer says, you let the customer know that you have absorbed and processed what the customer is saying.

Seek ways to turn a transaction from "you versus me" to "you and me versus the problem". This can be accomplished by saying things which take on the customer's agenda as your own, such as "I'll do what I can to resolve this," and by making it clear that you serve as that customer's advocate to your organization.

With just a small amount of effort, an enlightened concern for the customer will help most transactions go much more smoothly, by replacing the implicit "battle lines" of the transaction with a sense of trust. More importantly, with practice, it makes these transactions much more pleasant on both sides. Many professional customer service experts value their jobs because they provide a "pat on the back" many times per day from customers. A well-developed sense of empathy is an important part of creating that environment.

These guidelines cover many of the most important aspects of working well with customers in a service situation. They are not at all independent of one another, but interrelate as part of a larger whole that constitutes one's basic stance towards the customer.

Staging: a powerful communications technique

Imagine two very different situations. In one, someone is simply asking a customer to pay a small fee that they forgot about. In the other, a dentist is about to put all sorts of scary things like needles and drills into the same person's mouth. Curiously, you may find that the dentist often has more success. Why? Because he or she is probably using a technique that is perhaps the greatest secret of communicating well with customers. We will call this technique *staging*, because it helps you break a potentially emotional situation up into smaller stages.

Staging is one of the most powerful methods you can use to gain the trust and cooperation of a customer. It is a technique that comes naturally to many people in high-contact professions such as medicine and law enforcement, where delivering good or bad news well is a necessity. In a customer service setting, the same technique will create a profound and very positive difference in how people react to you.

Staging involves a three-step process:

Step 1. Introduce what you are going to say before you say it.

Step 2. Explain what you are saying as you are saying it.

Step 3. Empathize with the customer after you say it.

For example, the dentist we mentioned earlier will probably tell the patient exactly what he or she is going to do, discuss the reasons for it, explain what kinds of things to expect, and then reassure any concerns that are voiced by the patient. As a result, the vast majority of people will cooperate with the dentist, rather than bolting out of the chair as an escaped dental patient. Unfortunately, many people neglect to do the same thing in a customer setting. The result is often a longer, more difficult transaction with misunderstandings on both sides.

Here is a simple example of how staging works. Let's say that you have just taken your car in to repair a minor rattle in the dashboard, and it turns out to be an unexpectedly expensive repair. Here is how many people would handle this situation:

You: I'm calling to check on the status of my car repair.
Them: Lemme see ... ok, sir, it's going to cost 800 dollars.
You: What?!!

What frequently happens next is that you react with shock, anger and mistrust, all of which is directed at the person on the other end of the line. You then become more and more angry, and the other person responds by becoming rigid and defensive, until you finally hang up the phone in a huff. Now, let's try this again, but use staging.

You: I'm calling to check on the status of my car repair.

(Step 1: Introduce)
Them: Let me see... ok, Mr. Jones, I have your records in front of me. It appears that you brought your car in because of a noise behind the dashboard. Since this sounded like a small matter, we were hoping that this would simply be a minor repair. Unfortunately, it turned out to be something more involved than that.

You: Oh, really?

(Step 2: Explain)
Them: You are probably aware that your car, since it is a late-model vehicle, has an airbag system. These systems are normally very reliable, but since they are sealed components, when something goes wrong with them, we are often required to replace the entire system. In your case, we found a broken connector in the airbag system.
You: How much is that going to cost me?
Them: These are unfortunately fairly expensive systems, relative to other components on an automobile. This particular system would require approximately $800 to repair.
You: Oh my goodness! That's almost two weeks' pay for me!

(Step 3: Empathize)
Them: I agree with you, this is an unusually expensive repair. I wish that this hadn't turned out to be the problem! But because it is an important safety item, I am glad that you brought it in. Would you like me to have you speak to one of our technicians to discuss your options from here?
You: Yes, I would appreciate that.

By this time, you will still not be happy, but there will be an important difference. Instead of yelling at the person on the telephone, you will probably be calmly discussing your options with them. They will have successfully turned a situation of "you versus me" to one of "you and me versus the problem." From there, both parties can move forward as partners to negotiate a solution.

A more subtle point is that the first person will probably go home at night complaining about these stupid customers that yell at him, and how it isn't his fault that their cars need expensive repairs. The person who uses staging regularly, doing exactly the same job, will think that her customers are just fine and that she has a great job. People often feel that customer reactions are caused primarily by the situation itself, and never realize what a strong influence that their own communications skills are. Of all these skills, using staging can be one of the key factors that create a consistently legendary service experience in any situation.

Staging works because it accomplishes several powerful things:

- It softens the blow of difficult situations by explaining them in detail.

- It tells customers that you are willing to take the time to discuss the situation with them.

- It provides data that people can use to help them accept or negotiate the situation.

- It provides a chance to build customer confidence and demonstrate your expertise.

- It allows you to speak to the customer's own self-interest.

Some situations require a little staging, while some require a lot. I will never forget the first time I ever boarded an airliner by myself, for a job interview in Seattle after college. First the flight was delayed, and then the next thing I knew, the cover was lifted off one of the plane's jet engines as mechanics swarmed all over it. A few minutes later, we were herded on board the airplane, we pulled back and taxied to the runway, and all sorts of scary thoughts were running through my mind about what might have been going on with that engine.

Shortly after takeoff the pilot came on the public address system and, in that reassuring drawl that pilots often have, welcomed everyone on board the flight. He then launched into a very detailed, technical discussion of what had been repaired on the engine, what role this component played, and how it was a minor problem that they wanted to make right. It didn't matter at all that I had no idea what he was talking about. The fact that he calmly explained in detail what was happening gave me the confidence to relax and enjoy the rest of the flight.

Staging sounds deceptively simple, but doing it well takes time and practice. It is not part of human nature, but a learned way of responding. When you make it one of your habits, you will find that people respond very differently to you then they have in the past. This is because you will have made the transition from reciting facts to demonstrating leadership in a customer situation.

Above all, the staging technique helps both you and your customer transcend the situation and become partners. (And I truly mean any situation – for example, one of the best examples of staging I have ever seen came when I received a large, unexpected tax bill, and the civil servant who answered my phone call left me almost glad to pay it by the end of the call.) It represents one of the most simple, powerful and cost-free ways to boost your service quality.

Delivering Quality Service on the Telephone

When Alexander Graham Bell first ushered in the era of the telephone by saying "Watson, come here, I need you" to an assistant in another room, he probably never envisioned today's world of millions of people communicating at the speed of light. Nor could he have envisioned waiting on hold, listening to bad music, or receiving busy signals. Nonetheless, telecommunications still represent one of the fastest growing means of customer contact. New advances in telecommunications technology have fueled more sophisticated telephone transactions than ever before.

Service by telephone adds a new dimension to responsive customer service: the need to convey a good experience to customers who cannot see you, or perhaps hear you either. Here are some of the ways you can sound good to customers on the other end of the phone.

Use an effective opening

The very first thing you say, and how you say it, sets the stage for how a customer will perceive the transaction. If the opening statement conveys a message of "Yeah, what?" it may steel the customer for a war of nerves and cause the transaction to be unnecessarily long and contentious. On the other hand, a greeting that conveys a sincere interest in helping the customer will focus their attention on working with you to solve the problem rather than dumping on you. Many firms have a prepared opening statement that tries to achieve these objectives. Some components of a good opening statement can include:

- Introducing your company and yourself by name.
- Asking the customer for their name.
- Asking how you can help -- ideally, using the customer name which you have just been given.

Turn over the floor to your customer quickly. Avoid being too verbose or too curt while aiming for a polite, sincere middle ground between these two extremes. For example, a good opening statement combining these elements might proceed as follows:

"Welcome to Super Software. My name is Rich Gallagher. May I have your name? (pause) Thank you, (customer name). What can we do for you today?"

Depending on your service environment, you may also ask for other customer information, such as an identification number from a service contract, or a date of birth for verification purposes. To do this politely without the appearance of a confrontation, phrase this in the form of a polite request, or provide some information about what you are asking for and why. Compare these two exchanges:

Service: XYZ Company.
Customer: I have a problem with my widget.
Service: Service tag number?
Customer: Huh?
Service: I can't help you without a service tag number.

These blunt requests set up a stance which implies that "You have to do what I say before I will condescend to help you." The tension that then results will not make the transaction easier for either party. This is a better opening style.

Service: This is XYZ Company. How can I help you?
Customer: I have a problem with my widget.
Service: I'll be happy to assist you with that. All that I will need from you is a service tag number for our records.
Customer: What's a service tag number?

Service: It's a four digit alphanumeric code that is on the back panel of your widget. Do you have that with you?
Customer: Oh, yes, here it is: ABC2.
Service: Thank you very much. Now, what can I do for you?

Here, using a good opening and follow up makes for a better transaction on both sides. Practice phrasing your openings and see how well they work in actual phone conversations. In time, you will gain a sense for what works best with customers. This kind of experience will help you adapt your own company's procedures to your own personal style of making a good first impression on the phone.

Control your tone of voice

Most human interactions include a lot of non-verbal communication. People note the way that you make eye contact with them, nod your head, smile, or cross your legs, and make judgments as to how you respond to them. On the phone, you are suddenly limited to verbal cues. In one sense, that's good, because you mainly need to control just one thing to make a good impression -- your tone of voice. In person, you might look people in the eye, nod frequently, smile, and say "uh-huh" once in a while. On the phone, people can only judge you by the sound of that "uh-huh".

How is your tone of voice? A simple test is to assess how people generally react to you on the phone. Do they get better or worse with you as time goes on? Even when people have problems, they usually react well to someone who seems to care about them. If your tone of voice on the phone could use a tune up, try the following tips.

- Make it a point to pause, then smile, before you answer the phone.

- Buy an inexpensive suction-cup telephone microphone and tape yourself speaking with a willing partner, not your customers – it's not only unbecoming, but illegal, to tape phone conversations without notification and consent of the other party.
- When you leave a message for someone, check if their voice mail system has the ability to review your message before leaving it. If so, use this as an opportunity for practice.

Aside from making sure that you sound pleasant and cheerful, practice sessions are a good opportunity to check mannerisms in your voice, such as poor diction or a sing-song pitch. Aim for a tone that is crisp, clear and well modulated. With time and practice, the habit of a better tone of voice can become automatic.

Put on your game face

In competitive sports, getting psychologically ready for the next game is often referred to as "putting on your game face." Years ago, when I worked briefly as a radio announcer, I noticed a similar phenomenon. Many announcers underwent a dramatic change of voice when they put on their headphones and microphones. People with whiny, nasal voices, whom you would never imagine being in radio, would suddenly speak in deep, resonant, clear tones on the air. Many people in that profession work to develop a distinct radio voice. Most people outside of the industry might be surprised to hear what their favorite media personalities would sound like if they were suddenly woken up at 2 AM!

In telephone customer service, one can also learn to develop a "customer" voice that is clear, distinct and friendly. You can use the same technique which media personalities do: learn to associate picking up the telephone with switching to this customer voice. Cues such as these help to reinforce good speaking habits and make a good phone manner come naturally.

Um, Um, Um

Many people have a habit of trying to fill gaps in their conversations with monosyllables such as "Um", "Er", "Ah.". In a sense, these phrases are a bit like snoring -- we all know people who do it but aren't aware of how much we ourselves do it. To the listener, these fillers can be irritating and unprofessional.

One of the most effective tips for dealing with these mannerisms comes from Toastmasters International, a popular public speaking organization. Their meetings feature a person serving as an "Ah" counter who rings a loud bell every time a speaker makes an extraneous utterance. It is remarkably effective. Speakers noticeably stop using these crutches as weeks go by, for fear of being "dinged", and the improvement is lasting. Try having a friend or loved one do the same with you some time, and you will probably be stunned initially at the number of times the bell rings, but as this exercise is repeated, you should notice a definite improvement.

Again, take advantage of message review features when you leave messages on other people's voice mail systems. Listen to the number of times that you utter an "um" or an "er," and then record and re-record the message until it is clear and free of verbal clutter. With practice, learning to consciously reduce to these mannerisms leads to crisper, smoother speech on the phone.

Silence isn't golden

Few things irritate customers more than the lack of a sense of closure about their problems. Particularly on the phone, long silences in response to a customer can create the impression that you aren't listening and don't care. Here are some ways to make sure that you "close the loop" with the customer by providing good feedback:

- Repeat information that you are provided back to the customer. This has the dual advantage of showing the customer you are paying attention, and giving you both a chance to clear up any misunderstandings, before action is taken.
- Be directive and action-oriented. Tell the customer exactly what you plan to do, and what they can do next if that doesn't help.
- Always tell customers to come back if they are still stuck.

When you provide closure to a transaction, it serves as a "receipt" to the customer that their words were heard and will be acted upon.

Slow down

Normal human speech is about 140 words per minute. When we are on the phone, it is easy to lose sight of how rapidly we speak. A calm, easy pace in the conversation helps put a customer at ease as well as gives them the opportunity to break in to the conversation and provide information. If you have a tendency to speak too fast, make it a point to slow down, and listen intently when you are on the line with a customer.

Sign off with a proactive summary

At a point of completion, close off the transaction by clearly setting out the action items from this call. Use active closing phrases such as:

"I'll be sending this order out today."

"Try this, and please let us know if there are any further problems."

"Once we receive your part, it should be repaired within two weeks."

Pause and allow the customer to agree to these items. If everything is agreeable on both sides, you can then end the conversation with a final closing statement. In some environments, there is a standard closing phrase that can be used; otherwise, a sincere, courteous phrase that thanks the customer for calling should suffice.

Beyond these techniques, perhaps the most important issue to handling customers on the phone is the attitude that you bring in to each transaction in the first place. When you feel a genuine respect for callers and their problems, many of the issues mentioned above become a natural part of the conversation. Conversely, when you can't wait for customers to shut up and leave you alone, such guidelines merely put a band-aid over symptoms of a much larger problem. The hidden payoff in telephone customer service is that when you adjust your job perceptions from getting rid of customers to making them feeling as good as possible, they tend to call less and spend less time with you on a call. The long way around is often the shortest way home.

Phone Call Practicalities

Beyond your personal style on the phone, there are also a number of more pragmatic issues that affect your customers' experiences. Here are some of the operational aspects in providing customer service by phone.

Managing returned calls

A great deal of time is often spent playing the game of "telephone tag" -- you miss someone's call, they leave a message, they miss your returned call, you leave a message, and so forth. These are some ways to return calls more productively.

- Call back during times when people are most likely to be in. For the usual 9 AM to 5 PM workday, the best times are normally 10 to 11 AM and 2 to 4 PM. Where possible, avoid calls too close to either lunch time or the beginning or end of the day.
- When you miss someone, and leave a message, suggest the best time to reach you. For example, "This is John Smith. You can reach me from 9 to 5, and the best time to contact me is anytime after 2 PM."
- Before leaving a message, ask when the person will return. This way, you can avoid messages and repeat calls for someone who will be gone for the rest of the week.

When you do finally get through to another party, remember that you may be one of a number of callers for this person, so proactively state the reason for the call. "Hello. I'm Steve White from Stereo Service returning your message about an amplifier repair." This puts the transaction back on track from where it was last left off and gives the customer a sense that you intend to help them.

Screening and escalating calls

When a customer calls in, minimize the amount of time that they spend with your organization by routing them to the right person immediately. Doing this well can range from having an automated phone system helping to channel the calls – "Press 1 for toaster problems. Press 2 for mixer problems." – to combining a good telephone receptionist with specific teams of people.

As an individual customer service professional, the most important aspect of call screening from your end is to know how to get people to the right place once you have determined their needs. This may involve either referring the customer to another resource or escalating it by transferring the call directly to another person or to a supervisor. Know in advance areas such as:

- Who has what kinds of expertise within your organization.
- What backup resources you can use when the target specialist is not available (other specialists, voice mail, etc.).
- What the procedures are for connecting the customer with another person, including what to do when the other party is busy, on the phone, or away from their desk.

In general, it is good to maintain a relationship with a pool of contacts, both inside and outside of your organization, to complement your own expertise. This way, when you receive a question outside of your own skill set, you can respond proactively and say "I work with a real expert on that at such-

and-such a company. I'll arrange for him to call you. If you miss each other, you can reach him at 555-5555."

Navigating your telecommunications system

Many of today's telecommunication systems can practically do everything but tie your shoes, with features including voice mail, interactive voice response menus, and document retrieval via fax. Using this to a customer's benefit requires keeping up with the features and functions of your particular system, and knowing how to put them to use where needed.

Most organizations will train their staff initially to use their phone systems -- the problem is, when features go unused for too long, they can become forgotten in the heat of a transaction. Make sure to keep current reference material nearby. Practice basic tasks specific to your system, such as how to transfer a caller into someone's voice mail box, how to set up a conference call, or how to send information to a customer's fax machine.

Today's era of automated telecommunications make handling the practicalities of a phone call have become every bit as important to the customer as your personal attitude on the phone. Callers today can tell horror stories of calls being passed from one clueless person to another, or being misrouted to voice mail systems that never let them connect with another human being. Worse, it has become easier to dump someone into an anonymous call stream where no one individual takes responsibility for solving their problem. Conversely, customer service professionals who become accomplished at using their telecommunications systems have the potential to benefit customers more effectively than ever before. Managing customer transactions by telephone is now both an art and a science – and an important area of expertise unto itself.

Quality Customer Service On-Line

Business transacted over the Internet, or "e-commerce" as it is popularly known, has become big business today. Within a few short years, many electronic retail pioneers have grown to become corporations with a greater market value than many of the world's century-old marketing giants. At the same time, competition has become more fierce in this arena than in any market in history, and for many firms service quality has become a key differentiating factor.

At the same time, consumers often rate the overall quality of service on the Internet as being very poor. Some of the most common complaints include a lack of response to electronic mail, the inability to reach a human being when there is a problem, and poor technical support when there are computer problems with shopping or ordering. Worse, in today's high-volume on-line service environment, there is a greater risk of receiving wrong answers or responses that don't address your questions.

Being on-line can magnify the impact of service quality on both your personal career growth and the success of your organization. As Amazon.com founder Jeff Bezos once noted, "It's an incredibly important success factor for selling on the Net, because unhappy customers don't tell 6 friends, they tell 6000. The Internet enables a free flow of information, which is great, but it makes it essential for an online retailer to offer the best possible service."[4] Nonetheless, many firms often struggle with even the basics of providing a good on-line service experience.

Once, I personally had a billing problem with an on-line service I was using – I had switched to a flat-rate plan the month before, but was still being charged by the hour. First, I tried to call them about it, but the line was constantly busy. Next, I sent them an electronic mail message. A week later, I got a form-letter response that explained the differences between their billing plans. I tried another e-mail, and a week later received another form letter response noting that I had signed up for the flat-rate plan.

Once again, I sent another e-mail, this time asking them to please stop, take a deep breath, and actually read my question – namely, why was I still being charged by the hour. Finally, a week later, I received a reply saying that they had discovered a technical problem affecting some people who had switched the day that I did, and that they would straighten things out. Overall, it took nearly a month to resolve the problem.

On the other hand, the electronic frontier represents an opportunity to provide better service than ever before, when it is managed well. On-line technology now allows people to respond quickly with a world of information that simply isn't available in telephone or face-to-face service transactions: for example, a customer can download a new version of your software, obtain pages of detailed product advice, or share experiences with other customers on an interactive "bulletin board." It can also be a highly cost-effective means to providing service to more people with less human intervention, and quickly reach a worldwide market. Managing these consumer experiences well represents a tremendous opportunity if you work or manage a business on-line. Here are some things you can do to help create a great customer experience in cyberspace:

Respond quickly
Electronic mail is not an immediate communications medium – it is more like regular mail than other media such as the telephone. When people communicate with you electronically, there is often an unspoken fear that their request will fall into a

black hole, to be addressed at some time in the far future, if ever. When you consistently provide quick responses to electronic mail, within the accepted business standard of 24 hours, you will encourage future use of this medium.

Don't over-use technology

It is more possible than ever to increase your service productivity by automating your responses to questions. These often become the electronic equivalent of a form letter. If you use them, however, you take on an even greater responsibility to make sure that you accurately diagnose each request and respond appropriately.

Value quality over quantity

On-line service environments make it easier to track productivity and service volume than ever before. Don't become so enamored of "keeping your numbers up" that you don't give each problem the proper attention it deserves. Cases such as the billing problem above highlight how the wrong focus on productivity alone can lead to the cyber-equivalent of "Let George do it" and create poor service experiences.

Leverage on-line resources

The Internet provides your customers access to a vast array of resources that wouldn't be available in a face-to-face transaction, such as account records, detailed product information, or related Internet sites. Make use of techniques such as links to appropriate World Wide Web pages or e-mail addresses, as well as attached computer files with programs or information.

Don't forget the human touch.

Some on-line responses are clearly written by thoughtful human beings, while others sound like they were composed by the KGB. When you can't see your customer, it can become too easy to be cold and emotionless in your replies. Always keep the customer's feelings in mind when creating on-line responses.

The growth of today's on-line community is nothing short of revolutionary, yet in many ways, customer service on-line is just like customer service in any medium. You are still judged by how well you satisfy people, solve their problems, and help them feel good about doing business with you. At the same time, it still represents a major frontier in commerce, and a permanent change in the way that customers interact with businesses. People who learn to create an excellent service experience on the Internet have a key competitive advantage over those who just view it as a technology.

Professional Customer Contact Skills

One point to be made about the techniques in this chapter is that they form the core of a skill set common to nearly every kind of customer service professional. In summary, here are the most important guidelines.

- Good customer contact skills are learned techniques that can be understood and practiced.
- Communicating well with customers creates shorter transactions, easier solutions, and happier customers.

- Good communication must be combined with effective action, expertise in your job, respect for the individual, and a genuine empathy for their needs.
- Giving a little more than expected is the defining trait of the most successful customer service professionals.

You might ask where the place of "attitude" is in all of this. Rest assured that it is there, but it is more than being nice. A professional customer service expert, accomplished at managing each transaction with the right kinds of communications skills, is displaying the ultimate in a helpful attitude. These techniques applied every day will benefit your customers, your company's reputation, future sales, and the employee's own skill level and job satisfaction. In short, everyone wins.

Step 2:

Create a Quality Service Experience

Communications skills such as the ones we discussed in the previous chapter are important, but legendary customer service involves much more than good communication skills. Beyond these basics, there are things that people say and do that form the building blocks of an excellent service experience. The good news is that these are things that you can learn and practice as part of your own personal service style. Some of these skills include:

- Learning what phrases to use (and avoid) to create a strong customer relationship.

- Controlling "negative expectation," the tendency to over-protect your interests instead of soliciting what is best for the customer.
- Practicing good non-verbal communication, in areas such as eye contact and body language.
- Above all, using the "105% rule" to manage your customer's expectations and then consistently exceed them.

If there is one common thread running through each of these techniques, it is that most of them are habits that can be developed easily with practice. They do not require the strength of Hercules, or a change in your personality, to work into your daily routine. At the same time, most of them transcend normal human relations – if you practice them and make them good habits, you will stand out from the vast majority of people who interact with the public. Here, we will look in detail at how to put each of them to work in your own daily life as a customer service professional.

What You Say is What You Get

An old joke among football fans discusses three people in heaven, talking about the bravest accomplishments of their lives. One man states that he saved his mother from drowning. The second says that he rescued his neighbors from a burning house. The third finally says, "I rooted for the New York Giants at Chicago's Soldier Field.". The others asked him when he had done that, and he replied, "Five minutes ago." Nearly everyone can tell a story about the consequences when someone said the wrong thing. Less often discussed, but equally important, is the strong positive effect of saying the right thing in many situations. Good customer relationships are often made -- or lost -- in small efforts that require little time. The most important of these revolve around what you say to people.

To treat customers well, one of the most productive things you can do right away is also one of the simplest. Learn the phrases that make people feel good, and become aware of the ones that make people feel bad. Phrases such as the ones that follow are easy, cost-free, and surprisingly effective ways to build a strong, positive relationship with the public. If you adapt phrases similar to the ten best listed below into your own personal style, and watch out for the ten worst, you will send the vast majority of your customers away much happier than when they arrived.

When you start using these phrases, you will reap two immediate benefits for yourself. First, your dealings with people will become much easier and friendlier. Second, and most important, you'll develop a first class attitude that will enhance your overall skills with the public.

The Ten Best Things to Say to a Customer

There are several things you can say to a customer that can make a big difference in how the relationship and the events of the day proceed.

"I'll be happy to"

When confronted with a customer request, you have a fundamental decision to make -- you will say yes, or you will say no. If that request falls within your responsibilities, it is likely that you will say yes. But the words you choose to phrase this yes could make your customer feel upset or feel great.

The presence or lack of enthusiasm makes no difference in how much work you do. If you enthusiastically agree to look up some information for a customer, or grudgingly agree to look it up, you are still going to look up the same information. Enthusiastic, affirmative agreement costs you nothing and gains you a great deal of positive attention, both from your customers and your management. If you are going to do something anyway, it costs you nothing to make people feel good about it.

Try an experiment tomorrow. Do exactly the same amount of work you normally do, but agree to everything with gusto. Get into the habit of saying things like "I sure can" instead of the usual "I can." When someone asks you to do something, respond with a heartfelt "My pleasure." Smile and nod a great deal -- even on the phone - when people talk to you.

At the end of that day, you will be amazed at how much fun you had. The work you did will seem less like work. People will respond to you better. If you continue this experiment over time, you may find yourself being considered one of the most talented, smart, and effective people in your company. The way you respond to people is one of those high-payoff items that costs nothing.

"That's a very understandable problem"

Many customers feel embarrassed about bringing their problems to you for help. In these situations, you have two goals: to solve their problem and to make them feel good for having asked you to solve it.

One major pharmacy chain built a recent television advertisement around this issue. A worried man comes in, paces around the pharmacy counter for a while, then asks the pharmacist in hushed tones about the side effects of his medication. After the usual commercial message, the ad returns to show the obviously relieved man thanking the smiling pharmacist. The implication is that people will shop where they aren't made to feel foolish for asking advice.

Psychologist Carl Rogers summarized this issue as his principle of unconditional positive regard -- to listen without judgment to what a person is saying, and respond empathetically to that person's feelings. Rogers was one of the first researchers in his field to show that the empathy a patient felt was at least as important a factor in getting well as the counseling techniques themselves.[5]

Putting customers at ease about their concerns is one of the fundamental ways of building that bond of empathy in your own work. Personally, whenever people tell me that they feel bad for bothering me, I always say, "Look, this my profession. I enjoy solving your problems. The saddest day of my life will be when no one calls or comes in anymore." And I truly mean it.

"I've had a lot of experience with that problem"

It makes people feel good to know that they are dealing with an expert. Put the opposite way, how would you feel if a mechanic took your car's engine apart, scratched his head, and said "Gee, I've never had any experience with these V-6's." What if you stepped on board a jet airliner, and the pilot timidly announced over the intercom that this was his first flight?

Believing that customers come first doesn't imply you must be humble and servile. In actuality, it's good to toot your own horn. Most of us prefer win-win situations dealing with equals who enjoy doing a good job.

Examples abound of the "healthy ego" that's part of a certain pride in what you do. Animators who drew Donald Duck cartoons for Walt Disney would show off by painting faithful reproductions of the great paintings of history, replacing the main subject with you-know-who.[6] Jet propulsion engineers from a major aircraft manufacturer once pitted their skills against the public in a paper airplane contest. Even the people who run Rhode Island's largest garbage dump offer picture postcards, tours, and at one point an evening lecture series entitled "Dinner at the Dump".

Look at the real estate section of any newspaper and you'll see many sales or achievement awards listed after people's names. Why? You'll understand the minute you set out to sell your house. You want that feeling of certainty that someone can get the job done. If you're great at what you do, never be afraid to let it show.

"I'll get you an expert"

Of course, you can't always call yourself an expert and mean it. Nor should you. If you are a good doctor, but not a brain surgeon, I do not want you to perform brain surgery on me. It's perfectly alright to admit an honest lack of knowledge as long as you keep your focus on finding the resources to solve your customer's problem.

One of the best responses in situations like this may be to consult with another expert for how to solve another person's problems – and perhaps learn from that expert yourself. When you smile and say, "I want to make sure your problem gets fixed right. I'm going to have our supervisor come talk to you," you are granting that customer a certain importance. Also a second opinion can open up possible solutions that might not have occurred to either of you alone. The Rev. Robert H. Schuller describes this kind of expert relationship as "linking-thinking," where the whole is greater than the sum of its parts.[7]

As you bring other people's resources to bear on a problem, remember that the best kinds of working relationships are often built around tooting one another's horns as well as your own. When a customer brings in a car with a leaky transmission, and you can truthfully say "I'll arrange to have Joe work on it. He's one of best transmission experts in the business," you are building a great relationship with both the customer and Joe.

"Here's what we will do"

Telling someone exactly what you will do for them, and when, leaves an important sense of closure to a customer transaction. You should never leave a customer wondering what will be done next for their problem.

A person's perception of customer service depends as much upon how you treat them as it does on raw response time. You might assume that people would be happier with an immediate response than with being called back later. All else being equal, this is true. However, years of running a telephone hotline has shown me that people are often happier with a pleasant referral than a surly on-the-spot answer!

I see this trait time and again in myself. When my flight gets delayed, and the ticket agent explains the situation, empathizes with me, and works hard to get me on another flight, I still feel good about the airline. But if I grocery shopping, and the checkout clerk scowls and curtly dumps my change in my hand without a word, I am angry at the grocery store. If I were to confront the clerk, I'm sure the response would be, "Well, I did my job and gave you your change, didn't I?" Yes, but if the clerk made me feel like a chump. I'm not as likely to return to that store.

The single biggest productivity tool in a customer transaction is to close by summarizing the action. Take the case of calling a ticket agency and the conversation goes flat.

Customer: I'd like two seats to next Friday night's opera.
Service: May I have your name, address and credit card number?
Customer: Here it is...
Service: OK. Thank you for calling.

This "OK" usually will not close the transaction but instead will probably result in a barrage of follow-on questions from the customer such as, "When will my tickets arrive?" "What time does the performance start?" "Could you verify that you got my address right?" "Let's make sure I'm being ticketed for the right event." It will also leave a bad impression with the customer and probably infuriate them if a mistake is discovered later. With a proactive summary, the chances are much better that the transaction will end quickly, pleasantly and free of errors:

Customer: I'd like two seats to next Friday night's opera.
Service: May I have your name, address and credit card number?
Customer: Here it is...
Service: Thank you, Mr. Davis. I've reserved two tickets in seats 31-F and 31-G for *La Boheme* at 8 PM on Friday night, May 12 at the Metro Concert Hall. I'll be sending them to 31 Lake Street, Smithfield, California 91234, and they should arrive by Wednesday. Is there anything else I can help you with, Mr. Davis?
Customer: No. Thank you very much!
Service: Thank you, Mr. Davis. Have a nice day.

Summaries are particularly important when there is a problem. In the case of the delayed flight mentioned earlier, the ticket agent's manner not only makes me feel better but also boosts their own productivity in the process. Because I am satisfied that the best efforts are being made on my behalf, I move along instead of arguing with the agent or demanding to see a supervisor. The person who understands what to say when a problem can't be fixed right away spends less time, and faces less anger, than the person who doesn't. It's important, above all, to fill a customer's need. At the same time, using a proactive summary to grant a customer the importance and empathy their problem deserves -- whether or not that need can be immediately filled -- is one of the true secret weapons that will make your work with customers easier and more productive.

"Can we do anything else for you?"

This is not always an easy question to ask, particularly with a difficult customer. Why? Because they might actually ask you to do something else.

Still, this ranks as one of the better cost-free ways to spread good feelings. It says that you care. Although 99 per cent of the time, the answer is, "no, I don't need anything else," almost everyone will think that it was very nice of you to ask. Since many customer service jobs are in busy, stressful environments where many people try to do as little as possible, your positive attitude will stand out in the customer's mind.

Another good reason to ask this is that it makes sure your customers are really satisfied. We are all prone to having a hidden agenda of what we really want, in spite of what we ask for. Computer users, for example, are often afraid to ask direct questions they feel might make them look ignorant. Asking if they would like anything more explained further makes the whole transaction easier for the customers without being pushy or invasive.

"Thank you"

Your job does depend on customers using your services. As corny as it sounds, saying "thank you" makes them feel welcome to return in the future.

The funny thing about thank you is that it's so widespread in our service culture that its absence stands out a great deal more than when it is said. Don't risk seeming rude by leaving out a pleasant send-off.

Many companies have their employees use specific phrases such as "Thank you for shopping with us." There is nothing wrong with official pleasantry, done with the right sense of style, and in the absence of a standard closing it is just as important to develop your own personal ways of sending people off with a smile. It might be a sincere "Thanks for calling," "Take care," the omnipresent "Have a nice day," or something completely unique to you. Either way, the right sendoff lets people know that you enjoyed helping them.

"Nice to hear from you again. How are you?"

How often do you hear this one? When you turn a faceless customer into a friend, the benefits are plenty. First of all, you've gained a friend. Second, you've made it much more likely that future problems will be handled with respect on both sides. Third, you've often gained a customer for life.

The amount of familiarity that you develop with customers will depend on the frequency of contact that you have with them. Either way, the same principle applies. If you work with random, faceless hordes every day, you can still welcome them warmly and treat them well. If you have more frequent contact with customers, however, it is important to understand the effect that regulars have on your business.

If a bank loses your paycheck, and you talk with an indifferent, anonymous bank teller about it, you're immediate anger is probably directed at the teller. If you talk with someone with whom you have a longstanding friendship, you're more likely to be mad at the bank. In fact, with a good enough relationship, you might even avoid being mad at all – provided that they do, in fact, find your paycheck!).

Use the customer's name

For most people, few things capture their attention better than their own name. The personal touch reaffirms one's sense of self and uniqueness in the impersonal, "Dear Taxpayer" world we live in. Moreover, it gives people the good feeling that, if you took the trouble to notice their name, you'll probably take the time to solve their problem as well.

You have an advantage here in situations like phone service, where customers often contact you first and give you their name. Write it down or type it in as you start speaking to someone. Even in person, you probably know more customers by name than you think you do.

When a customer hands you a business card, or a credit card, you then have the ability to say, "Thank you, Mr. Davis." When someone at the office refers a customer to you, you can get their name from your co-worker and greet them by name when you first see them. And when someone has a meeting with you, have your receptionist and support staff greet them by name.

One person who will always stand out in my memory is Liz, the receptionist for a Southern California computing firm. I would call and ask for someone, and she would connect me. By about the third time I'd called, she would greet me with "Hello, Rich! I'll bet you're looking for so-and-so." By then, I didn't even have to identify myself -- she'd recognize my voice and greet me with small talk.

Over the years, my contacts with the company became more sporadic. At times, more than a year would go between calls, yet every time, I would be recognized and made to feel welcome by someone who had never even met me. That company, which receives hundreds of calls per day, is gifted with someone who adds a rare personal touch for its clients. There is no question that it adds to their reputation.

"Come back if you need more help"

In the opening scene of the Walt Disney movie *Lady and the Tramp*, there is a quotation that says, "There is one thing that all the world's riches cannot buy -- to wit, the wag of a dog's tail."[8] In the same manner, no amount of effort on your end will ever let you usurp the customer's right to judge whether their needs have been satisfied.

Telling someone to come back if they need more help affirms the truth that it's their right and not yours to declare the transaction completed. It's one of the nicest ways to send off a customer.

The Ten Worst Things to Say to a Customer

Most of us could come up with a very long list of the "worst" things to say to customers, and the majority of these would probably involve some degree of rudeness. I suspect, however, that you and I are not rude people -- we are, of course, nice people. Going on this presumption, this section is a summary of the worst things that nice people say to customers, things that you and I could say if we aren't careful.

"That isn't my job"

One of the worst things that could happen to your career, whether you are in the mailroom or the boardroom, is to fall into the trap of, "That isn't my job." If you plan to be a success in a public-oriented position, your job is to send people away happy whenever and however possible.

It is a very tempting statement to make. If you work in the men's department of a retail store, and a customer asks you for help in the adjoining toy department, it probably isn't your job. You may not be able to ring up the customer's purchase even if you want to. Nonetheless, the customer is much more interested in having his problem solved than he is in your job description.

A good response to this situation is to offer to get someone from the toy department, and pick up the phone and page them. Better yet, go and find someone yourself. It is never acceptable to tell them that it isn't your department, and walk away. What you say is of equal importance to what you do. If you truly cannot assist the customer, make sure that what you say is oriented towards what will be done to solve their problem -- even if what you do is cheerfully linking them up with someone who can do the job better.

More to the point, examine carefully what you can do for people within the bounds of your job. In the years I have spent managing a software support hotline, we have gladly handled everything from financial contract issues to restaurant reservations for customers. One even called me asking how to spell *Szechuan*, so he could find a restaurant in the phone book. For that matter, if someone had called up wondering what to do about a sick elephant, we wouldn't have sent them away without at least a couple of phone calls in search of a good elephant veterinarian. A good rule of thumb for almost anyone is the can do attitude -- if you can, do.

"Did you read the manual?"

If they did, it's an unspeakably rude thing to say. Even if they didn't, it certainly doesn't make you seem eager to help. Instead, be positive and suggest exactly where they should look -- and better yet, if it doesn't take too long, answer the question as well.

The phrase "read the manual" has become a stereotype, particularly in fields such as consumer products and computer software. It tells us how too many people on the outside see these companies' view of service. A recent joke in the software business goes, "How many computer programmers does it take to change a light bulb? None -- it's a hardware problem." Like any stereotype, this one tangibly hurts growth and business. In my mind, the "read the manual" attitude of expecting people to know everything in advance ranks right up there with "that isn't my job" as career poison.

There are some situations where the customer should have done a lot more homework, or is even totally beyond help. We'll discuss these cases later. Consider them as the rare exceptions that they are.

"You don't understand"

Here is a variation of the old saying, "The customer is always right": if someone doesn't understand you, it's always your fault -- even when it is their fault.

You have to be particularly careful on this point, because when you are the expert on something, many legitimate questions will seem dim-witted, and people will seem slower to grasp things than they should.

If you are a mother or a teacher, you have a head start at understanding this issue. Answering questions takes kindness, patience and a time-honed skill at finding different ways of explaining things. Take your time, keep an even tone of voice, and smile as you try to get your point across.

"I don't know what I can do about it"

This is the phrase that angers me the most when I hear it. What makes it even more frustrating is the fact that many people in the habit of saying this could do something about it if they cared to.

The same comments for "that isn't my job" apply here as well. Your focus should be on the customer's problem and not your potential lack of expertise. A very positive way replacement statement is to say, "What would you like me (or us) to do about it?" This empowers customers to tell you exactly what they would like, which enables you to give a direct answer.

"What do you want?"

This doesn't refer to the rude, "Whaddya want?" borne of annoyance. Rather it is the implication that the customer is somehow interrupting you and perhaps shouldn't have. Even in the most pleasant tone of voice, asking what customers want puts them on the spot.

Always put yourself at people's service. Emphasize your willingness to help rather than their problem. Replace "What do you want" or "What do you need" with phrases like "What can I do for you" or "How can we help you". I once worked for a gregarious Texan who never answered a phone call without saying "Can I help you?" in the same breath as his name. It's a nice touch that I've since taken on myself, and it puts people immediately at ease that they aren't bothering me.

"You'll have to call us back"

Why don't you or your company offer to call them back?

I will grant one tiny exception to this issue. There are businesses that, as a matter of course, do not return long distance telephone calls for cost reasons. (These companies should hope that they never have competitors who do.) If you are in the position of working for such a firm, the burden is on you to politely explain the company's policy, while emphasizing how important the customer's problem is to you.

"You're all set now"

It's natural to feel that you've solved a customer's problem. That appraisal, however, should come from the customer, not you.

It's alright to say that something should fix a customer's problem, especially if you invite them to come back if they need more help. But if you are too presumptive, however, it will seem that you are impatient and anxious to get rid of the customer.

"That's an unusual request"

For most people, telling them they are different from everyone else makes them feel stupid and insecure.

Some professions use this fact to their advantage. You make a reasonable offer on a new car, and they laugh at what a ridiculously low figure it is -- just to make you feel bad enough to offer more money. The problem with taking this mentality into normal customer transactions is that putting someone on the defensive instantly vaporizes any rapport between you.

The key here is to separate your personal feelings about the customer from your mission, which is to send that person away satisfied. It is perhaps too easy, when a customer seems like a pain in the neck, to find ways to transmit this evaluation back to the customer. A better approach is to make it a matter of personal policy never to evaluate your customers, unless it's in the form of a compliment to put them at ease.

In the example of the car dealer, there is an incentive to try to deflect a customer's request by pointing out that it is different. Unfortunately, when it succeeds, you've often deflected the customer as well. A better approach with unreasonable requests is to politely defer, and blame it on yourself: "I'd love to sell you that car for $200.00, but my manager would shoot me. Would you like me to see what kind of a price I can get for you?" In general, honesty is the best policy. But above all, don't pass judgment on your customers.

"I have no idea"

No one person knows everything, and it is perfectly OK to admit your ignorance. What you should avoid at all costs is to do so and then leave the customer hanging about what to do next. Here are two ways to handle this situation.

Not so good:

Customer: Where can I purchase rocket fuel for the Space Shuttle?
Service: I wouldn't know.

Better:

Customer: Where can I purchase rocket fuel for the Space Shuttle?
Service: I'm not sure myself, but let's see if we can find out for you. Have you tried talking to NASA?

Customer: No, I hadn't thought of that.

Service: I'll try to find their number for you ... Hello, Cape Canaveral directory assistance, can I have a phone number for NASA? Thank you ... OK, here's the number. Have a nice day.

Since every situation is different, we all must make judgments about how far we ourselves should go to help someone in a difficult situation. The key point here is to guide people, whenever possible, to the next step in solving their problem.

Silence

Silence isn't golden in the field of customer support. Silence translates to inaction in the mind of the customer, and being too low-key is seen as rude.

Suppose that you walk up to a bank teller, hand him your life savings of $50,000, and ask him to deposit it. He then says nothing, gives you no receipt, and then calls for the next person in line. Do you walk away satisfied? More likely, you want to grab this person by the tie and demand a receipt, to make sure your money is deposited correctly.

In the same way, an answer from you serves as a verbal receipt. It tells the customer that you heard them, and what your response is. Moreover, liberal feedback allows both you and the customer to be sure you understood each other. You avoid the situation where your customer wanted two plows and instead receives two cows.

Always be directive and action-oriented. tell the customer exactly what you plan to do, and what he/she can do if that doesn't help.

How to Always Say the Right Thing

Examples such as the ones above serve as reminders of things to say and not say. At the same time, they point out a greater sense of style in how you deal with customers within your own specific profession. If you develop habits of speech along the lines of the ten best things just discussed, the chances are good that you'll naturally avoid falling into the trap of saying phrases like these ten worst ones. Your basic stance towards customers, day in and day out, is a great source of influence on what automatically comes out when you open your mouth.

> One day my wife and I went to an auto garage selling a promotional flashlight for four dollars. We bought one, but discovered when we got it home that it required an expensive lantern battery instead of regular flashlight batteries. When I took it back and asked for a refund, the manager first refused, then changed his mind and handed me the money with a great deal of annoyance. When I told him that I appreciated it, he said angrily, "Yeah, I bet you do."

> This garage is not only four dollars poorer but also lost our business, permanently. To this day, we go out of our way to have our automobiles serviced elsewhere. Ironically, if I had even been refused the refund politely, we would probably still be using their services.

Too often, our response to people is governed by our feelings, instead of our thoughts. Someone bothers us, so we react automatically with annoyance. Another person feels we fouled up, so we instinctively defend ourselves instead of fixing the problem. The problem with feelings is that they offer little guidance in responding to people.

Instead, transactions with customers need to be practiced and managed in much the same way that one might manage their cash flow or production schedules. Understand the most common situations that you are likely to encounter in dealing with the public, learn the most appropriate ways of dealing with these situations, and then practice them until they become a habit. Had this garage owner better understood his best response to the standard refund situation, he would have been much less likely to shoot from the hip and lose our business.

Common phrases such as the ones above represent more than good guidelines. With practice, they become part of a style in which saying the right thing becomes more automatic over time.

Start introducing some of these phrases into your daily work with customers today, and see what a difference it makes. You will, in all likelihood, be very pleasantly surprised at the change that it makes. Most importantly, you will be taking a positive step towards developing your own personal skill set for providing excellent service to people.

Avoiding "Negative Expectation"

Deep down inside, most of us feel that we are nice people. At the same time, it is easy for us to become blind to what we instinctively say to people when they present us with a problem: we have an innate urge to protect ourselves, rather than help the customer. Understanding this instinct, and using this knowledge to change the way we interact with people, represents a critical turning point in developing a strong customer focus.

I recently experienced this phenomenon first hand when my home computer needed repairs under warranty. I was eventually instructed to take it in to a local computer store to have it fixed, and when I arrived there with computer in hand, the discussion went something like this:

Me: Hello. I'm here to get this computer fixed.
Them: We don't service this kind of computer here.
Me: But I was told by the warranty firm to bring it here.
Them: Oh ... well, we do fix those computers for that company. But they have to fax us an authorization form before we can work on it.
Me: They did fax you an authorization form. Here's a copy I brought with me.
Them: Oh, I see...

He finally summoned a technician, who told me that the store had in fact had been expecting my computer, and promised me it would be fixed the same day. But when I called back late that afternoon, the woman answering the phone responded, "When did you bring it in? Today? It wouldn't be finished that soon." However, when I asked her to actually check, sure enough, the computer was ready.

Do you see a common denominator in these conversations? It's a phenomenon known as *negative expectation*. A customer presents you with a problem, and you respond with a list of all the things that you can't, don't and won't do. It then becomes the customer's responsibility to steer the discussion back towards fixing the problem. The focus is on your agenda, not the customer's.

Negative expectation happens so often because it's a part of human nature. Early in life, we learn to deal with the world's ceaseless demands by setting limits on what we will and will not do for others. The problem is that when you bring this human nature into a customer service setting, your priorities end up in the wrong place. Worse, you risk infuriating people when you use it in cases where you aren't correct – for example, I am certainly not going to rush back to patronize this computer store in the future. Here are some ways to avoid setting negative expectations.

Ask questions first
In the example above, the people at this computer store were so busy setting limits that they didn't take the time to assess what I wanted. In general, when you get that tingling urge to tell customers what cannot be done, that's a signal to slow down, ask lots of questions, and be sure you understand the customer completely.

Paraphrase the customer
By interpreting and repeating what you hear from the customer, you have an opportunity to make sure you understand each other before you start making judgments on their requests.

Check things out
Give people the benefit of the doubt and check out what they tell you, before you start making assumptions.

Help proactively, limit reactively
When you can offer a benefit to a customer, speaking up ahead of being asked is the mark of a professional. Conversely, when you need to set limits on a customer's expectations, the customer should drive the process.

My wife and I once had a weekly habit where I would buy her a hot fudge sundae at an ice cream shop – but being health conscious, she liked it made with frozen yogurt rather than ice cream. Almost every time I came in, I would order the sundae, and the proprietor would reply with a dour "Frozen yogurt is 50 cents extra." This happened so often that I became tempted to say "I'd like a hot fudge sundae with frozen yogurt and yes, I know, it's 50 cents extra" every time I came in. It seemed like their focus was on constantly making sure that I understood their prices, rather than on making me feel welcome as a customer. Eventually, the shop went out of business.

Perhaps the most effective way to avoid negative expectation is to examine how you see your customers in the first place. If you see them as people who interrupt you, annoy you and demand too many things, and you react in kind, your perceptions will probably not be disappointed. On the other hand, if you start to see them as the lifeblood of your business and treat them as welcome guests, the need to set limits often drops dramatically – and when you do need to set limits, you will find that these situations can be managed using good communications skills. Try expecting the best from people, and see what a difference it makes in your customer relations.

Body Language and Non-Verbal Communication

In face-to-face customer situations, your success depends upon a lot more than what you say. Compare getting help from someone who appears stern and cold, versus another person who is relaxed and helpful. Even though both may do exactly what you ask, there is a big difference in your perception of service quality.

Moreover, a person's body language can have a great influence on how the overall customer transaction goes. When someone acts chilly towards you, you may not trust or accept what they say – which can in turn lead to longer transactions, more work, or even escalation to a supervisor. Conversely, a friendly demeanor can go a long way in resolving a situation quickly and professionally.

Non-verbal communication carries a lot more weight than most people think. By managing it well, you can add a substantial boost to your customer skills. In most situations, your physical reactions matter every bit as much as what you say.

> One day, my wife had to go to the emergency room at our local hospital. She was frightened and uncomfortable, sitting perched on the examining table waiting for the doctor to come in. Once the doctor arrived and saw the look on her face, he did something I've never seen a physician do before. Instead of standing over her to ask questions, he hopped up on the examining table to sit next to her, and bent down towards her, like an old friend, to listen intently to what she was saying. Before long, she had calmed down considerably.

Perhaps a simple definition of good non-verbal communication is to interact with your customers the same way that you would with your friends and acquaintances. At a more detailed level, we can break this down into four specific kinds of behavior.

Eye contact

Looking away from people is a classic sign of disinterest. (Conversely, too much eye contact, such as staring, will make people equally uncomfortable.) By making it a point to look at people in they eye regularly when you speak with them – particularly when you first address them – you will demonstrate interest and empathy, which in turn will help the transaction move forward successfully.

Facial expression

Smiling at customers has become a cliché, to the point where customer service workshops in the business world are often referred to as "smile training." Yet it remains one of the single most important ways to build a bond with people, particularly in difficult situations. A sincere smile conveys a willingness to help, demonstrates respect for the customer, and defuses anger.

Keeping a smile on your face is only the beginning of a good facial expression, however. You could smile all day at people and still create a poor impression on them, because your face can mirror a wide range of emotions.

Try an experiment sometime: stand in front of a mirror, and smile. Now try arching you eyebrows. Next, let out a sigh. Finally, smirk to one side. Would you feel you were getting good service with expressions like that? Probably not. Therefore, your goal is to maintain an open, positive, natural expression in front of the public. With practice, this look can be one that you naturally adopt when people first approach you for service.

Stance

How you react physically to the customer makes an important impression as well. Since prehistoric times, we have used our posture to protect ourselves or welcome others, and today our basic physical stance still conveys the same kinds of messages. Cues such as raised shoulders, crossed arms or putting our head down sends a signal that we are trying to close ourselves off from customers, while an open, relaxed stance invites communication.

Proximity

Every culture has an unspoken standard for how close two people should be to each other in normal conversation. (And it does vary between cultures; sometimes when two people from different countries are speaking together, one person keeps moving closer, and the other unconsciously keeps moving steadily backwards!) Normally, the best thing to do is follow the lead of your customers and remain close enough to demonstrate your interest.

Techniques like these become part of our own personal style with people. For some people, good non-verbal social skills come naturally, while for others, things can improve a great deal with insight and practice. Either way, they work in conjunction with each person's specific personality to create our own unique way of interacting with customers.

Normally, it makes sense to employ both good verbal and non-verbal communication skills to create a positive customer relationship. (There is one exception to this rule - there are situations, fortunately rare, where people of the opposite sex can mistake professional courtesy for personal interest. In these cases, trust your own judgment, and know when to back away.) However, the vast majority of customer transactions will benefit strongly from the right kind of body language and facial expressions, together with your good communications skills.

Your Secret Weapon: the 105% Principle

Handling customer transactions well has many dimensions. Much of what separates the best people in this business from everyone else boils down to a single, very simple philosophy: when your customers have a reasonable expectation to a certain level of service, give them what they expect, plus a little bit more. I refer to this principle as the 105% rule.

Does this sound like just another way of saying work harder? Not quite. Hard work, important as it is, is almost beside the point. The real issue here is managing, and then exceeding, people's expectations. The trick behind the 105% rule is to set realistic expectations and then exceed them at least a little. People aren't accustomed in this culture to getting even 100 per cent of what they wanted in the first place. Far too often, they're happy when they get even 80 per cent. So when you give them a little more than the minimum required in your job -- not necessarily a lot more, but even a little more -- it stands in stark contrast to practically everyone else.

Management expert Ken Blanchard once devoted an entire book to this concept: his bestselling Raving Fans tells a fable where the hero discovers a shield, which eventually reveals a message about learning what customers want and then delivering it to them "plus one."[9] In the real world, this simple concept forms the core of what can put you above your competition, whatever you do. Note these practical examples of giving 105% in customer situations.

- You need to refer a customer to someone else, and instead of telling the customer to call Mr. Smith, you offer to arrange for Mr. Smith to call the customer.
- You've just solved a tough problem for a customer, and you say "I enjoyed getting that fixed. Made my day."
- You take care of someone's problem, but then spend some extra time explaining exactly what you did.

Perhaps a key point here is that none of these examples necessarily involve putting in large amounts of extra work. They may simply be small, incremental efforts that may add no more than a few extra seconds to these transactions. Whatever effort you choose to invest, great or small, can be viewed profitably along the lines of an investment in the success of the customer, your organization and yourself.

Companies recognize the 105% factor as a big plus in their reputations. You can see it in their advertising. Years ago, a magazine advertisement for one major airline showed a gate agent leaping over a row of seats in the boarding lounge. It goes on to tell a true-life story of how the gate agent returned a passenger's briefcase just before his flight took off. At a more personal level, however, the 105% rule is an effective means of making customer transactions go smoothly: the old adage to "kill them with kindness" really does work. We can see this in ourselves. How do you feel when you come in to a store with a problem, you are full of defenses, and then they do more than you asked? Your emotional battle armor melts away, you work with them to conclude the transaction quickly and professionally, and you come away wanting to do business with them in the future. Sometimes, practicing this rule can have an very tangible payoff.

> I will never forget the time, early in my own career, when a university professor in our field imposed upon me for a favor. His school was buying a large amount of computer graphics equipment, and they wanted my advice on what to purchase. He would have been happy if I had simply called him back with a few ideas. Instead, I decided to spend part of my weekend providing him with as much information as I could, as a professional courtesy, for what would be an important purchase for them. I wrote and sent him a lengthy report describing the various kinds of equipment, what to look for, and where the industry seemed to be heading.

I had all but forgotten this exercise a few months later when I received another letter from the professor. He was now in charge of an international project to send visiting technical experts to universities in the People's Republic of China, and was wondering if I would be interested in an all-expenses-paid trip there to teach computer graphics. That trip was the experience of a lifetime, and the first in a number of international speaking engagements.

While the side effects may not be this profound or direct, one thing seems to be invariably true for almost everyone: providing a level of service which exceeds expectations, even a little bit, is a cornerstone to one's reputation for excellence with customers. I personally feel that the 105% rule is a simple principle that all but guarantees excellent relations with your customers, not to mention your company, the public and even your family.

A more typical example in my case was a situation where one of our software customers needed a problem fixed for an important management presentation. There were all sorts of problems, and the error was not resolved until the evening before the big presentation. Eventually, things ended up with me personally staying at work until 10 PM, driving the fixed product to the airport, and finally calling the customer at home in bed and telling him what flight the software would be on.

We didn't win the Nobel Prize for this evening of extra effort. However, the customer was sufficiently impressed to become a long term customer of our company and to write a nice letter to the company's president expressing his thanks for all of the effort that we had put in. The most important side effect was really measured in the long-term, cumulative effects of a customer base, which doubled in size every year during my five-year tenure.

One further point in applying the 105% rule to your professional toolkit is that doing it really well calls for a little bit of homework on your part. If you work for an organization, it is good to know what kinds of resources you have to solve a customer's problem in advance.

For example, some firms allow front line staff to resolve problems up to a certain dollar limit without consulting a manager, while others may simply trust their people to exercise good judgment and good business sense. When customers call with computer problems, it may not make economic sense to send each of them another free computer, but it does make sense to know how much budgetary or merchandise authority you have in solving problems effectively. Know your limits so that you can balance serving customers well with the financial realities of your company's product or service.

The 105% rule is one of the least understood principles of success in almost all areas of endeavor. For example, as a hiring manager, I have always noted that because so few applicants display a genuine interest in the job itself, people with even a little bit of interest really stand out, and are much more likely to get hired. Similarly, companies that provide even a little more care or service tend to get repeat business. Companies successful in the service arena often seem to prosper as much from sweating the small details as they do from grand differences in products or services. Putting forth 105 percent in your own working environment today will yield a guaranteed return on the investment.

Creating Service Leadership

If there is one core concept behind each of the ideas discussed here, it is taking a leadership role in creating a good service experience for each and every customer. Most people simply react to customer situations, while people who deliver legendary customer service treat them more like small performances in which they are the principal actor. And much like acting, the more time you invest to hone and perfect your craft, the better the performance will be. Techniques like the ones presented here are building blocks that you can use to create a great performance in any customer situation.

With practice, your communications skills and service skills become part of an overall style with customers, and this style in turn determines the image that you and your organization present to the world. When someone is described as being "customer focused" or having "a great attitude," it is often a matter of having developed these skills to where they become part of their nature. And when an entire organization commits to learning these skills, this style becomes part of its reputation, and more often than not, part of its growth rate and market share. These skills represent not only good customer relations, but one of the easiest and most cost-free ways to become successful in both the marketplace and your own personal career.

Step 3:

Handle Difficult Situations With Class

We are all difficult people. Every single one of us. This side of sainthood, we all have a threshold beyond which we become upset and unreasonable. Unfortunately, this means that as a customer service professional, you will at times encounter people who are beyond that threshold. Understanding how to work with people who are angry or difficult to deal with is perhaps the most important skill in a customer service professional's toolkit.

If every customer was happy all of the time, there would be little need for customer service. By definition, working with the public means solving other people's problems, and a significant proportion of people who have problems are not happy. At the same time, with practice one can see these unhappy people for what they are -- an opportunity to show off your best stuff. There are techniques that work in handling difficult people and angry situations. Few skills give you as much confidence as the ability to become a human "bomb squad" capable of defusing these situations.

In this sense, customer service work shares something in common with emergency service professionals such as police and paramedics. All of these groups need to develop skills at working on the spot with troubled people. For one of our best friends, a patrol officer who gets involved in situations ranging from auto accidents to shooting victims, one thing is constant: in a crisis, she and her colleagues know exactly what to do without a moment's hesitation. While the stakes are hopefully lower for most customer transactions, the approach remains the same. Understand how to manage the situation, put your skills to work, and bring the situation to a peaceful conclusion.

How to Defuse a Hot Situation

When someone becomes upset in a customer transaction, it is rarely a completely random, unforeseen occurrence. It usually follows a predictable pattern when a customer is not satisfied with a situation, and there are responses that can be used with a fairly high degree of success to both (1) lower the urgency level of the situation, and (2) negotiate a conclusion.

The best way to handle a customer confrontation, of course, is to prevent it from ever happening in the first place. Be careful to avoid displaying the kinds of attitudes and responses which might goad someone to react angrily, such as:

- Indifference to a customer's legitimate concerns,
- Lack of a direct response to someone's questions,
- Focusing on your procedures rather than their problems, or
- Not closing the transaction with positive feedback.

If you look back on the times when you yourself became upset in a customer service transaction, you probably felt the confrontation was their fault and not yours. In the same sense, most people become angry when they feel that they are being ignored or treated unfairly. Learn from this and give people the kind of service that you yourself would expect in a similar situation.

Unfortunately, different people have different thresholds at which they feel wronged, or vent frustration. Sometimes, they may respond inappropriately, either because of a misunderstanding, or perhaps the nature of their personality. For these cases, you need to practice techniques that will defuse the situation, and help bring the transaction to a peaceful close. With this in mind, let's look at some of the key principles to follow when you are face-to-face (or phone-to-phone) with an unhappy customer:

Stay Calm

Perhaps the most important skill in keeping a hostile situation on track towards a solution is to keep cool and not get drawn into the emotional situation that your customer is trying to create. While not easy at first, this becomes more automatic with practice. The key thing to keep in perspective is that you are a professional, and with experience, can handle situations like this as a normal part of your work.

Part of the problem with these kinds of customer transactions is that we expect anger to be associated with a certain personal closeness. You expect close friends and relatives to express strong feelings and argue with you, but where do these total strangers get off blustering to you about their problems? In return, your natural, innate response is to take it personally, and respond in kind. Yet this anger isn't directed at you at all. The customer is angry about their problem, and perhaps your organization, but generally not you personally. You could be Sir Winston Churchill or Bozo the Clown and they would still treat you the same way.

Within this fact lies one of the keys of defusing a complaint -- never make it personal. Keep the focus on that neutral, inanimate problem they are complaining about. Hate the sin, but love the sinner. Approach the transaction as though you were a sociologist studying frustration levels in people, and correctly consider their barbs to be extraneous to the situation at hand.

The most effective way to defuse the emotional content of a confrontation is to respond factually, and keep the focus on gathering the facts of the situation while working towards a resolution. Fact-gathering is not only important in its own right but also serves to temporarily divert the customer from their hostility while you try to solve their problem. Look at the following example.

Customer: This computer crashed in the middle of an important project! You people are all idiots! Can't you make a product that works right?
Service: I'm sorry that you ran into a problem. Tell me a little more about what happened.
Customer: I was in the middle of using my spreadsheet, and the screen suddenly went dark.
Service: Was the light on the front panel of the computer still on?

Customer: Er, yes. But I never could get your stupid screen to come on again, so I eventually shut off the computer and lost all of my data.

Service: I have a suspicion what the problem might be. Let me show you the back of this computer -- your monitor plugs in here, and if that cord gets pulled by accident, it can come loose. This is a very common problem...

Note that, besides gathering the necessary information, the service technician doesn't question or refer to the customer's state of mind or level of anger. The focus is on what might have happened, just as would be the case for a less angry customer. More importantly, the technician also takes the important step of focusing equally on the customer's real concern, namely how his data might be recovered.

There are two benefits to this kind of impartiality. It helps defuse the customer's own anger, and makes it much easier to get to the eventual solution. In the above example, if the problem was caused by the customer's dog chewing and tugging at the monitor cord, the technician's non-judgmental manner makes it easier for the customer to accept that this problem was self-inflicted. Similarly, if the problem was the fault of the product, this same calm manner helps you work with the customer to get it repaired with as little further venting as possible.

Above all, your goal in these transactions is to gently shift the customer's perspective from "you versus me" to "you and me versus the problem". Present yourself as an ally in resolving the situation by calmly servicing the transaction: acknowledge that the problem is a problem, empathize that you don't like problems like this, and then move forward from there towards a resolution.

Solve the Problem

There is no question about it: when someone is really upset about something, by far the most effective way to take care of that person's anger is to solve whatever they're upset about.

When it's Christmas Eve and you've just missed your connecting flight home to your family, all the politeness in the world means little compared with getting you on another flight home for the holidays. When someone fouls up your order for the second time, even the biggest smile in the world won't take the place of getting it right the third time. And when you're in the hospital, getting well ranks way up there over cheerful doctors and nurses.

The personal aspects of dealing with customers are very important. That is why this category gets equal billing with staying calm. Your personal skills make all the difference in the world in how one remembers the airport layover, the order foul-up or the hospital stay. But, never forget that you must fix the problem, and the sooner the better.

Make Up for the Problem

A certain percentage of problems that you encounter will involve situations, which are clearly the fault of your organization, and you must be prepared in advance to know what can be done to make a situation right. How you handle these situations has a large effect not only on customer reactions, but your organization's customer retention in general.

I wear eyeglasses, and one year I went to a major optical chain and replaced my scratchy old ones with a new pair in the same prescription. They looked great, they fit well, but there was one problem -- every time I wore them, I got a headache. I went back to this store with these glasses, and they tried new lenses. They still gave me a headache. I went back again, and asked if I could exchange them against another pair. No, I was told, now it's been too long, and they can't be returned.

So much for dealing with them again, I thought, and the matter ended there until much later that year, when I came across a promotional folder from the same chain. On its cover was a message from the company's vice president, stating their company's total commitment to customer service. It stated that if you've ever had a problem with their chain – past or present -- to write to him personally. I took up the challenge and wrote to this vice president explaining what had happened. Within a week, a phone call came from the manager of another store in the chain, asking me to see him personally. Upon arrival, my glasses were examined by both him and the head of the optical lab. After at least a half hour of tests, they returned and explained in great detail why these frames weren't suited to my prescription. The manager then selected one of the most expensive frames in the store, made another pair on the spot, and handed them to me at no charge.

Although I felt wronged, their response had so much class to it that this chain has gained my solid loyalty as a customer.

In comparing an experience like this to your own professional customer service work, the important thing is to understand how much latitude that you have to recompense or rectify common customer problems. Similarly, it's good to know when to get your management involved for cases which go beyond normal procedures, when you feel some kind of action on your organization's part is warranted. Taking a proactive role in making amends for customer problems is an effective way to avert or defuse hostilities from the customer, and generally makes good overall business sense as well.

Provide alternatives

Many a customer temper tantrum is caused by your not being able to provide what they want. Whether it's the last seat selling out on a non-stop flight, or your restaurant deciding to take fettuccini alfredo off the menu, it is inevitable that you will be in a position of having to say no to a customer. In cases like this, it's good to imitate what many good parents do with their young children. Point out the alternatives that remain and the benefits of these alternatives, then give the customers the opportunity to decide what is best for them.

Be aware that you will often face resistance from people who want what they originally had in mind, and be prepared to deal with this. Handling this situation well generally involves acknowledging the customer's concerns, politely repeating the alternatives, and then turning the floor back over to the customer to make a decision. Look at the example mentioned of a restaurant dropping fettuccini alfredo from the menu (to me, an unpardonable offense).

Customer: I'll have my usual plate of fettuccine alfredo.
Waiter: I'm really sorry, but we recently changed our menu, and we don't serve it anymore. Is there anything else that we can get you?
Customer: I can't believe that you folks would drop your fettuccine alfredo! I've been coming here every Thursday for this for the last five years. That ruins my whole evening.
Waiter: I know, that dish certainly had its fans! Unfortunately, our diners these days seem to prefer lighter, healthier entrees. There are some really good new dishes on the menu, though. I tried the new chicken parmesan myself last week and it's fantastic.

Customer: Can't you make a special request to the chef for me for a plate of fettuccine alfredo?
Waiter: I'm afraid that even if we could, we'd have to send out for the ingredients! I'll tell you what, though: if you would like to try a new dish, and you don't like it, I'll be happy not to charge you. Would you like some suggestions?
Customer: Oh, all right. I'll try some of that chicken parmesan.

In a case like this the waiter's patience and aplomb defused what could have become an encounter with an upset and boorish customer. Generally, every customer service professional can do well to take on some of the traits of a good salesperson: taking the needs of your customers, and then fitting them to the realities of the situation with as much class as possible.

Never Embarrass an Angry Customer
While it is important to keep your own personal bearings in a confrontation, it is even more important to preserve the customer's own dignity. A customer may not remember your customer service skills in a transaction, but they will certainly remember how you made them feel, for a long time after the problem has been resolved.

When we had a new home built a few years ago, it was plagued by just about every problem imaginable – floods, delays, builders who didn't show up, rising interest rates -- you name it. Practically everything that could go wrong did go wrong, as weeks and months dragged on. If, like me, you view yourself as an even-tempered, reasonable sort of person, I highly recommend having a new home built to experience first-hand what it feels like to be an angry customer.

Eventually, the situation came to a crisis in two crucial days. My mortgage commitment would expire for good unless I had a certificate of occupancy on Wednesday. To get one, I needed to complete one last detail – the home's floors and carpets had to be installed by Tuesday. I had called the carpet store the week before and received their commitment to install the flooring on Tuesday. But when I showed up on Tuesday, the person in charge had gone on vacation, and no one else there had a clue about my floors.

Now, if you wanted to see a livid customer, you should have been there. I stood there demanding at the top of my voice that they reach this guy, demanding they do something, demanding that the person behind the counter personally get those floors in that house. In the end, they did take care of the problem. The floors were finished at the last minute, and soon I was sitting in a finished new house with my name on the mortgage. However, the next time I came into that store after that, a couple of salespeople rolled their eyes skyward and said to each other "Well, if it isn't Mr. Gallagher again."

On paper, the store did a good job. They did get my house finished on time. Yet because of a few comments by those salesmen, I was too embarrassed to go there ever again, and the substantial amount of money I later spent on home improvements was spent elsewhere. It may seem hard to blame those salesmen – after all, I was unreasonable. However, a few kind words to let me know that it was all right, that lots of people are upset when new homes are at stake, and I would have been a repeat customer. And keeping a few personal feelings more private would have translated to more commission dollars in their pockets.

The moral of the story is: Never make enemies that you don't have to. Not only that, but go out of your way to soothe the hurt, embarrassed feelings that are a part of every hostile transaction. Remember that each of us can be an angry customer, and that every angry customer has a reasonable side as well. When you make an angry customer feel like a valid, worthwhile human being, the rewards will come back to you many times over.

Take an Interest

Perhaps the crowning touch in customer service is taking someone who is visibly, absolutely upset with your company and turning them into a friend and customer.

Bill was a regional sales representative for a heavy equipment manufacturer. He was used to hearing "no" on his periodic sales calls, but he was quite unprepared for the torrent of abuse that came from the purchasing agent at one company. "Don't even think about calling here! We want nothing to do with your company. Now go away and leave me alone!"

Many, if not most, salespeople would come away and say, "Well, I guess that means NO!" But Bill took this as a bit of a challenge. He waited a few days and then called the purchasing agent. Bill said, "Look, I'm not interested in selling you anything. I'm new in this territory, and you certainly seem upset with my company. I was wondering if we could get together sometime for a few minutes and discuss where we went wrong. I'd like to make sure that we treat our other customers better in the future."

The agent agreed to the meeting where he went over a long list of problems. The last salesman from Bill's company didn't keep delivery promises, there were shipping delays, and even quality problems with the merchandise when it arrived. Bill nodded and listened with interest, taking notes all along, and thanked him sincerely for his time.

Back at the office, Bill got on the phone with a number of officials at company headquarters, explained the situation, and made a number of recommendations. After reaching a suitable deal with the company, he then wrote a letter to the purchasing agent, addressing each of his complaints in turn. "My company is offering to ship you a large order at 50% off if you'd like to try us again. Also, we'd like to have one of our top technical people fly out to spend a week at your plant to solve the ongoing problems. And here's what my company's done in the last six months to become the industry leader in on-time shipments..."

Bill hoped that the offer, and his ongoing support, might bring back the customer – which it did. However, a pleasant and unexpected surprise was when that customer became one of Bill's biggest purchasers over the next year.

Get Help When You Need It

For most people, there will be times when your own efforts will not be enough to solve a customer's problem. Particularly in situations where a customer is agitated, it can make sense to bring in other parties with more authority or more expertise.

For example, let's say that a customer wants a refund for a defective piece of merchandise, and your company's policy only provides for an exchange. If you feel that the customer's request is legitimate under the circumstances, but you don't have the authority to provide the refund, the best thing to do might be to get your manager involved. On the other hand, if you know for sure that no amount of management intervention or outside expertise will give the customer what they want, it's time to go over the remaining alternatives as discussed earlier.

There is a deeper issue here as well, of taking what you learn from these transactions and trying to improve your own organization's policies and procedures. If you face frequent customer wrath because of your store's return policy, or need management intervention on a regular basis, your experiences might be valuable feedback for your company as a whole -- particularly if you come armed with ideas for a better way to do things.

Smile

Some of the most subtle but important points in a confrontational transaction are your body language and facial expressions. Appearing confident and helpful can often be one of the quickest ways to take the wind out of an angry customer's sails.

When we are tense or upset, we naturally tend to adopt certain physical mannerisms: our shoulders tense and raise up, our face tightens, and our expression becomes grim. It's a good idea to pause every so often during the work day and check our own physical stance. Push the shoulders back down, take a deep, relaxing breath, and smile.

More importantly, keeping customer problems and behavior in perspective helps deal with the emotional factors that drive our physical reactions. When my wife and I ask our friend the police officer how her day went, she might casually, "We tended to an attempted suicide today, made an arrest, and reported to the scene of an accident. Where do we want to go for dinner tonight?" She isn't devoid of feelings about these incidents, but accepts them as part of a day's work in her profession. This sense of perspective helped her to respond to people with the professional demeanor that one expects of a police officer. A similar perspective towards typical customer behavior helps make your professional customer service work easier as well.

When Things Get Out of Hand

So you've kept a smile on your face, asked all of the right questions, presented the alternatives, and responded empathetically, and the gentleman across from you is still bellowing at the top of his voice and pounding his fist on the counter. Now what?

Start thinking about the end game for a transaction that has ceased to be productive. Here are some techniques that you can use when things get out of control.

- Practice fogging, the repetitive technique of calmly stating and re-stating the facts of the situation until the belligerent person runs out of steam.
- Keep throwing the ball back into the customer's court by pointing out what options are available, and then asking the customer to choose what to do from here.
- Take the customer's name and address, and offer to look into the problem and get back to them later. Then do so, after the heat of the moment has passed.

Only in the most extreme cases should you have to use your worst-case solutions: hanging up the phone, calling for the next customer, or in the extreme, calling a manager or security guard to escort the customer off of the premises.

I remember witnessing one example of perfect timing one night when an obviously drunk patron was trying loudly and unsuccessfully to get a room at a fully booked hotel. The desk clerk tried to explain things with aplomb and courtesy, and find alternatives for the man, but he was too inebriated to be reasoned with. Soon, a visiting policeman overheard the commotion, stood beside the man in full uniform, and said "Can I help you?" The drunk suddenly didn't need any more help, and left immediately.

A good customer service environment should have procedures in place to deal with the worst cases of abusive customers. It's best to have these kinds of plans understood between whole customer service team ahead of time. If you manage a customer service group, make it clear that you and the rest of the team will back up anyone who gets into a tough situation. At the same time, recognize these situations as the rare cases that they are. Managing transactions calmly and professionally in the first place can go a long way towards keeping the extreme cases as few and far between as possible.

The Hidden Payoff of Angry Customers

There is a paradox in dealing well with difficult customers. Very often, when you give your most arrogant, obnoxious customers the 105 percent treatment, they become your strongest supporters, the kind of people who write your president, become repeat customers, and treat you well in the future. These people often put you in what I would call "hero or goat" situations. If don't satisfy them, you are a goat -- part of the reason for the failure, in their eyes. But if you come through for these people, you truly are a hero.

People with pushy, demanding personalities often are not used to getting good service. Their very nature brings out the worst in people they deal with. They are internally braced for the worst when they contact service people like yourself. So when you give them great service, kindness and empathy, are they ever surprised! This surprise, on the part of enough people, is what leads to a great reputation for you and your company.

Managing other difficult customer personalities

Not every difficult customer situation involves people who get angry. There are challenging personalities in any business, and particularly in customer service. Fortunately, with the proper techniques, most of these situations can also be handled with class. Here is a look at three more of the common personalities you are likely to encounter in a customer transaction, and how to manage them.

The talk-a-holic

Once I hosted an on-line conference about customer service situations with a major interactive service, and one of the most frequent questions from the audience went something like this: "I work in a retail store, and am stuck behind that counter while someone talks on and on to me. They'll talk about their kids, their pets, their gall bladder surgery, and anything else that is on their minds. Then I can't break away and serve other customers. How do I get out of situations like this?"

Encounters with people who talk incessantly are often a big drain on your time and resources. They leave you caught between the desire to be polite to the customer and the need to do your job productively. Fortunately, they are also among the easiest customer problems to manage, when you use the right approach. Here are the golden rules:

Break in. People often wonder if they should interrupt someone who is constantly talking. The answer is that you must interrupt them – but there is a right way and a wrong way to do it. Most people simply butt in and start talking business again, at the risk of embarrassing the customer and creating a defensive transaction on both sides.

Instead, use a technique known as the *acknowledging close*. In it, you acknowledge whatever the other person is talking about, and then gently pull the discussion back on topic. Compare these two approaches:

Without an acknowledging close

Them: ...so you see, I was going to get out on that boat one more time and try to get some more fishing in...
You: Excuse me, sir, but we need to wrap up this credit application. Now, may I have the address of your primary bank?

With an acknowledging close

Them: ...so you see, I was going to get out on that boat one more time and try to get some more fishing in...
You: You know, Steve, I envy you – it seems like the fish are never biting when I go on vacation! By the way, I just need to get a little more information for this credit application. May I have the address of your primary bank?

In the first case, you are likely to create an adversarial relationship, while the second approach builds rapport as you get things back on track. When you consistently use an acknowledging close, even though it may involve a few more words from your end, you will frequently move a transaction forward much faster than someone who does not. It works because it helps create a bond with the customer, from which you can then get down to business more effectively.

Use binary "yes-or-no" questions. When someone is prone to being talkative, you can help them close the transaction sooner by phrasing your questions to have one short answer, such as "yes," "no," or a piece of information such as the person's name or telephone number. These are binary questions, a mathematical term for something that has an either-or response. For example:

Not good

You: What do you think of these colors?
Them: Well, let me tell you ... when I started shopping here three years ago, you had many more colors. Even my grandmother thought that the color selection was better back then. Then about a year later, around the time that you started that new promotion...

Better

You: Which of these colors would you prefer?
Them: Blue.

The right kinds of questions then give you an opportunity to jump in and take control of the situation again. When you hear that one-word answer, it's your cue to jump right back in and move the transaction further along, with the next binary question. Done with courtesy and class, you will be perceived as being interactive rather than abrupt, and will maintain good feelings on both sides of the transaction.

Use "closing" statements. This is perhaps the most difficult part of dealing with a talkative person. Most of us are conditioned to receive at least a tacit "permission" to end a conversation with another person, and many talkative people have never learned the subtle skill of granting this permission.

Here, you must help them by using "closing statements" that facilitate a way for both people to end the discussion gracefully. Examples of closing statements include:

"Thanks for stopping by."
"Well, I've enjoyed talking with you today."
"Let me know if you have any problems with this."
"We'll see you soon!"

Have several of these statements ready, because you may need to use more than one of them to get some people to wind down the conversation. Eventually, however, most people will respond to a polite overture to close the transaction and move on. (And in extreme cases, consider techniques such as the "bathroom close", where you must excuse yourself visit the rest room!)

Most talkative customers are genuinely nice people who react well to being treated professionally as customers. By using techniques such as the ones above, most of these people will feel that you are paying close attention to them, and providing responsive service. Handled well, the vast majority of encounters you have with your more verbose clients will end on a positive note, with both of you parting as friends.

The "over-my-head" customer

No one would dream of handing the keys to a jet airliner to someone with no flight training, or offering a test drive of an automobile to someone with no drivers license. Yet every day, customer service professionals are asked to help people who don't have the aptitude or training for what they are doing. In some cases, these people may require more help than you can legitimately provide within a service transaction. When this happens, your job is to steer these people to the right resources while protecting their own dignity and self-confidence.

The computer revolution has perhaps become a watershed for these kinds of problems. Tales abound such as the one about a person walking into a computer store, picking up a mouse, clicking it towards the screen, and then angrily demanding to know why the remote control didn't work! You cannot deliver a quality service experience when someone like this expects you to teach him how to manage his finances on-line that night. Unfortunately, this is a situation where the growing affordability of computers has surpassed their ease of use for many people.

The same can be said for many other products and services that require a certain level of skill on the part of the consumer. This means that in situations like this, you must set the proper expectations to be fair to everyone. Here are some tips for how to handle these situations:

Refer people to the right resources. The first step when customers are over their head, or demand too much, is to refocus it from being a problem to an opportunity. Discuss what would be required for the customer to have a good experience with your product, such as training or experience, and then sell the benefits of these resources. Finally, provide them with the information they need to find these resources.

Protect the customer's dignity. There is never a good reason to question or criticize a customer's competence. Follow the dictum of "hate the sin but love the sinner," and use emotionally neutral phrases that describe the situation and not the person. Compare these two approaches:

> **Not good**: "You don't have the skills to use this yet."
> **Better**: "There are some excellent training courses for people like yourself, who are brand new to computers and need to learn the basics. Would you like to see some information on them?"

As customer service professionals, it is much more productive to manage situations than it is to judge people. By keeping your focus on the situation and not the person's shortcomings, you are much more likely to create a good experience on both sides of the transaction.

Know when to set limits. The golden rule here is to decide whether you can deliver a quality service experience. If you can make a customer truly happy by spending a little extra time helping him or her use a complicated product, by all means invest the time. If that extra time is going to only frustrate the customer further, then it's time to change your focus to whatever will make the customer really happy, such as a simpler product or a training course, and sell its benefits.

When someone is less than knowledgeable, extra care and patience is required to create a good customer experience. By focusing on benefits, and how to obtain those benefits, you go a long way towards turning a difficult transaction into a positive one. Moreover, even the most uneducated consumer is still your customer. When you keep your own priorities on how best to serve them, you greatly increase the chances of gaining and keeping their business.

The never-satisfied

There is a saying that "everything is negotiable." Unfortunately, some customers take this sentiment to heart, and use their dissatisfaction as a weapon to try and get what they want. These are the people who want a bigger discount, a second helping, or an early bird special two hours later. To them, nothing that you propose is acceptable, and they will grind away at you trying to get what cannot be attained. Here, it is important to differentiate between people who unhappy for a legitimate reason, and people who will never be satisfied with any legitimate solution.

When someone is unreasonably demanding, one of the best approaches to handle the situation is to use a four-step negotiating process:

1. Ask them what they want.
2. Acknowledge their concerns.
3. State the limits of what can be done.
4. Go back to step 1.

Then repeat steps 1 through 4 until the problem is either resolved, or escalated to someone with more authority to resolve it.

By using all four steps, while being pleasant but firm, you demonstrate empathy while not allowing the customer to intimidate you into an unfair resolution. Eventually, most people will eventually negotiate a face-saving solution for both sides, or simply give up. When this happens, you will have succeeded because of your showing respect for both the customer and yourself in a difficult situation.

Difficult customer transactions: a learned skill

For many customer service professionals, their greatest fear is the fear of the unknown. They feel they have no control over the behavior of a customer, and feel helpless when confronted by difficult people. In reality, these people fall into a small number of well-known personality types, and the good news is that each of these personalities can be understood and managed within a customer transaction. Moreover, by doing your best to serve all customers well, you reduce the chance that situations will get out of hand in the first place.

There is an important economic payoff to handling difficult customer situations professionally. Although less than 5 per cent of all unhappy customers even complain in the first place, and fewer still become difficult to deal with, their reactions may be shared personally with a dozen friends or even millions of people on the Internet. With the right approach, as many as 95% of these customers will return to do business with you if you solve their problems, while a similar percentage will stay away if you do not. Numbers like these can often spell the difference between profit and loss for many companies.

Ultimately, there is an even greater payoff learning how to take good care of your least favorite customers. That is the confidence and skill that it gives you dealing with the rest of your customers. When you feel prepared for the worst cases situations, it makes it much easier to handle the more common, everyday transactions that form the bulk of professional customer service work. Remember that the difficult customer represents an opportunity for your professional development. Handled properly, many of them will join the majority of reasonable customers by transaction's end, with a little help from you.

Section II:

Team Skills

Step 4:

Manage a Service-Driven Team

When I speak to audiences about customer service, I often joke that I could call ten different customer service centers, and then after I've hung up the phone, tell you exactly how each of them are managed. There is a very close relationship between the leadership culture of a customer service team and the service quality it delivers. As a result, you cannot fully discuss legendary service quality without examining how to manage it.

What sets apart managers in the best customer service organizations from managers who grumble about how they can "never find any good help"? Perhaps it's a belief that their employees are hotshots, talented people who are valued, and know that they are valued. When you put your employees first, they will put you first as well.

More than anything else, your skills as a manager have a dramatic effect on the experience of your customers. Compare these two examples.

Dr. Martha Rogers of Marketing 1:1 in Stamford, CT tells of a person who once came into a bank with a request and was told by a teller that he would need to see someone who wasn't in. He then asked to have his parking validated, and the teller explained that she couldn't validate his parking without at least one transaction – company rules. He persisted, but she could not be budged. So finally, this customer, the chairman of a Fortune 100 company, made a transaction. He withdrew all of the $1.5 million dollars from his personal account, and never returned.

One day I was personally shopping at a Wegmans supermarket, and there was a sale on toilet paper: three rolls for the price of two with their discount card. Problem was, I'd forgotten the card. I shrugged, put two rolls in my cart, and forgot about the matter until I reached the checkout. The clerk noticed this and mentioned the sale, to which I sheepishly replied that I'd forgotten my card and that it was no big deal. It was apparently important to her however. Within seconds, a swarm of people were at work looking up my card number in their records, changing the price, and running to the other end of the store to bring me another roll of toilet paper.

The customer service staff in both of these examples were doing exactly the same thing: trying to please their bosses. The difference was that one was managed to follow rules, while the other was managed to encourage repeat business. As a result, one lost a customer while the other has won over my business despite a competing superstore right next door. Multiply these incidents by the hundreds of thousands of transactions which take place every second, and you have what makes many companies succeed or fail in the marketplace.

Resources abound in most companies for information about the nuts and bolts of management, such as planning, budgeting, and scheduling. This chapter takes a closer look at more personal day-to-day concerns of people who work in customer service management: setting goals, improving employee relations, preventing burnout, encouraging growth among your people, and team-building. These areas are closer to the true goals of management than its pencil-and-paper aspects because far too many people today can turn in a monthly budget report but cannot motivate a team of customer service professionals. Conversely, people who can think big and take their team along with them frequently reach their goals, and have fun doing it.

R-E-S-P-E-C-T

Let's start with what is perhaps the most important success trait of any manager. Many employers think that their staff is primarily motivated by how much money they earn. They aren't. In reality, most people are motivated by how much respect they feel on the job. Respect goes far beyond good feelings, into being perhaps the key factor in your team's productivity, turnover and service quality. Creating an atmosphere of genuine respect for the individuals on your team is perhaps the single most powerful thing you can do to create a service-driven environment where you work.

Respect is one of those virtues that sound obvious in theory, but putting it into practice every day requires a concerted effort to make it part of your organization's culture. Here are some of the key ingredients for making it happen:

Sending the right message

As a manager, probably the single biggest factor in your organization's service quality is literally sitting right under your nose: what you say to, and about, the people on your team.

If you lined up most managers and asked them if they respect their employees, most would say "yes." But if you listened in on some of their day-to-day discussions, you might hear things like complaints about subordinates, impatience with people's limitations, and grumbling that "we can never find any good help." Instead of getting people to buy into a common goal, they bark orders and make demands ("after all, it's their job, isn't it?").

Managers who truly respect their employees start from a very different place. They hold people to high standards, and expect them to be met. But they coach and counsel people instead of bossing them around. They recognize and appreciate a good effort. They listen to different opinions and interact with people. Most importantly, they share the big picture of their organization's goals with the team, and let their team help lead the way to meeting them.

Treating people as individuals

On a job, everyone needs to meet certain core performance standards – perhaps coming in on time, or meeting certain levels of productivity, and above all doing their best to satisfy your customers. Beyond these core standards, each person has a unique personality and their own individual strengths and weaknesses.

One of the most subtle and misunderstood aspects of respecting your team is how you treat their unique talents. Too many organizations expect everyone to be the same, and criticize the weaknesses of people who don't completely fit their stereotype. The most respectful ones seek ways to get everyone to play to their strengths.

In my own experience managing software customer service operations, I have always seen a mix of talents. Some are very good listeners, others are technically sharp, and still others have talents such as good organization or attention to detail. Since no one person is ever good at all of these things, the key to success is to get everyone doing what they are best at. Customers who need a lot of patience and hand-holding are steered towards the good listeners, ones who need expertise are put in the hands of our technical hotshots, and critical issues get put in the lap of the people I can trust the most to follow through.

This process is similar to what championship baseball teams do. Some players are good starting pitchers, while others specialize in getting left-handed batters out in the eighth inning. Some are great hitters, while others may have a low batting average and play excellent defense. By using each of these people where they fit best, the whole team wins the game. By combining high standards with a team-based pool of resources, you too can get everyone "pitching innings" in the process of delivering a consistently good service experience.

Dealing with mistakes

One of few guarantees in life is that everyone will make mistakes. How you respond to these situations is a key indication of your level of respect. If you focus on punishing mistakes – and worst of all, if you do it publicly – you are all but guaranteed to foster a culture where people are more concerned with fixing the blame than fixing the problems.

A colleague of mine once worked as an airline employee. One day he finished fueling a jet airliner, got into the fuel truck, and drove away as he had done thousands of times before – only this time, he had forgotten to unhook the fuel line from the aircraft first, and the truck jerked to a halt. An inspection by the pilot revealed serious damage to the wing of the plane, and my friend had to watch thousands of his company's dollars go down the drain as a full load of passengers were deplaned and the aircraft taken out of service.

He went to his management expecting to be fired – but instead, he was told, "We know that you are one of our most reliable employees, and we are sure that this won't happen again." By showing their faith at a critical time, this company sent a strong message of respect, and saved itself from compounding its loss with the loss of a good worker.

Encouraging frank and open discussion of mistakes has benefits that go far beyond showing respect for people. It helps the whole team learn from where things go wrong, encourages people to take the right kinds of risks, and gives people an honest chance to improve their performance. Most importantly, when customers have legitimate complaints or grievances, it helps your people focus on making things right rather than protecting themselves from blame.

Recognizing good performance

Every person has job requirements that they are expected to meet. But when someone consistently goes above and beyond these requirements, particularly to serve a customer, they are in a sense handing you a gift – a gift that should be acknowledged if you want to receive more of them in the future. Good organizations celebrate their successes, and the people who create them, in ways that range from formal recognition to a sincere "thank you" to key contributors.

Valuing the whole person

People are much more than their work, and each person is a unique individual with their own family, culture, interests and dreams. Workplaces made up of homogenous groups who disdain "outsiders" or favor "insiders" not only border on discrimination, but often serve as hotbeds of poor service and lost market share as well. By respecting the diversity of your workforce, and treating everyone with equal dignity, you send a powerful message that you value top performers from any background.

Perhaps the best argument for creating a culture of respect is your own self-interest. When each person feels like an important, recognized and unique member of the team, you build an environment that not only breeds success, but returns that respect by putting the interests of the organization at heart. In a very real sense, mutual respect helps every person become managers unto themselves, and multiplies your own leadership efforts across every member of the team. It is one of the most important and cost-free building blocks in making the transition from hard work to legendary customer service.

Keeping In Step with Your Troops

At the same time that management requires leadership and vision, it also requires you to remain close to the activities of every member of your team. While some people may feel that being a manager puts you above the day-to-day activities of your employees, nothing is further from the truth for most effective customer service managers.

Ellen Dudley manages the customer service center at NEC Business Communication Systems in Syracuse, NY, a supplier of telecommunications for critical environments such as hospitals, hotels, schools and even correctional institutions. Here, service has to be much more than a smile. When Mother Nature knocks out the phone service to a major hospital, lives may be at stake. Yet as you walk around their auditorium-sized call center, with blue lights flashing and call statistics scanning across message boards, there is an underlying sense of good humor and camaraderie. And her team is very good at what they do. It isn't unusual for agents to coordinate nationwide parts and service resources to get a customer back on the air in the middle of a storm, in the middle of a weekend.

When asked the single biggest factor is in her success as a manager, without hesitation she replies, "I can perform any job in this organization myself." She explains that maintaining her own expertise is important not only in running the operation but in sending a message to her employees. "In order to ask someone to perform a task, I have to be able to perform that task myself. And if I'm given a new area of managerial responsibilities, the first thing that I do is learn it, even if it means a stint as a dispatcher or technician. I feel that this is really important, because you can't understand the frustrations that people might have with their tools or their situations if you haven't done it yourself."

Beyond building respect within your group, there some very practical advantages to pitching in with your customer service team.

Keep your own decision-making skills sharp

If you've been on the front lines juggling problems with the rest of your team, you aren't as likely to promote rules or procedures that make your staff's life more complicated. Instead, you will see the world through their eyes in making your decisions and be better able to champion the group's agenda to the rest of the organization.

Serve as a resource

When you take a senior role in a group, the buck stops with you. Being able to jump in with your team when it's called for underscores your willingness to do whatever it takes to provide great service. This becomes no less true at any level of management. For example, when Debbi "Mrs." Fields visits one of her chain-wide cookie stores, she doesn't just point out quality problems; she goes back into the kitchen and helps people get it right.

Set an example

According to NEC's Dudley, her active role makes it possible to maintain the high standards her organization requires. "The people who work for me realize that I know what I'm talking about, and that I can empathize with what they're doing because I've been there. And at the same time, they realize that we're running a business here, and when I ask people to work hard I can honestly tell people that I'm not asking them to do what I wouldn't do myself."

There is one school of thought that specifies that you can learn all about management, and then apply this management to whatever needs to be supervised. Another school of thought espouses that you can't, for example, run a baseball team if you haven't stared down a batter with a full count. I personally would strike a middle ground on this point. One can find both examples of successful supervisors who came up through the ranks as well as successful supervisors who brought in a great deal of outside depth and knowledge. But to be successful, all reached a point where they understood thoroughly and absolutely what they were making judgments on. When it comes to customer service, you need to know -- and that means really feel, in your gut -- what quality service is. Then reward it.

Start With a Goal

Psychologists describe two kinds of people: task-oriented and goal-oriented. Task-oriented people see things in terms of the process. If you tell them to paint a house, they look at their job as moving a brush up and down for eight hours a day. Goal oriented people seek instead to beautify the home, and plans their activities accordingly.

People in leadership positions need to be goal-oriented. If you observe the daily life of a physician, you might conclude that their job consists of writing prescriptions, giving injections, filling out insurance paperwork, and scheduling office staff. If you ask them what their job is, however, you might get the answer, "My job is to save lives." In the same sense, when I was a customer service manager, I never described what I did in terms of submitting capital equipment proposals or attending planning meetings. My job, pure and simple, was to help create the best level of customer service in our industry.

The importance of starting with a goal first is that it guides everything else that you do from there, and gives you benchmarks to work towards. More importantly, when you share these goals with your team, it harnesses the efforts of everyone on the team to reach these goals.

It is also important to segue your goals with the company's goals. The term *segue* has its roots in the music field; it means starting a song or program so that it blends smoothly with the end of the last one. Success as an orchestra conductor or radio personality often depends on doing clean segues. Likewise, your company has overall goals for itself – and if it doesn't, it should. Your goals must segue cleanly with those of the company for both parties to succeed:

- If the company goal is to become the sales leader in a competitive field, plan the kind of service that will keep customers coming back.
- If the goal is to introduce people to an entirely new kind of product or service, look into what kind of an educational role you can take.
- If your company is out to rebuild in a down economy, look for creative ways to cut costs.

No matter what business you are in, you are part of a team that must pull together. If you find that your personal goals are at cross purposes with those of the people you work with, clear the air and come to agreement on a direction you can all work on together.

Goals are the big picture in vertical communication between levels of an organization. Even the vice-president of General Motors has goals from the president of General Motors, if they expect to work effectively. They are the messages, which go between a manager and his or her group. Above all, keep your goals front and center, in the eyes of both you and your group, in your daily plans and decisions.

Ask the Experts

Now that you've thought about how messages flow from the top down, realize the equal importance of information that flows in the other direction, in the feedback managers get from their employees. Many management theorists believe that the people who do a job are the ranking experts on how to do that job. Are you wondering how to improve productivity on the assembly line? Ask the people you have working on it. Looking for a way to control maintenance costs? Have your maintenance professionals make some recommendations. And, of course, the most qualified experts on your customers are the people on your customer service front line.

Unfortunately, too many work environments today are from the top-down, where managers from above tell people how to do the work and how to fix the problems. But increasingly, industries are recognizing the bottom-line impact of giving employees a say in the operation: in many manufacturing plants today, for example, any worker has the authority to stop the assembly line when they spot a problem. This trend is important not only from a standpoint of getting the right input to make decisions, but also from one of fostering a sense of professionalism and expertise among people to get the best from them. After all, do you feel good about your work when someone tells you precisely what to do and never listens to you?

Nurturing individual participation is an important component of turning employees into experts. Doing it well is both an issue of personal style and organizational policy. The former involves having your door open and meaning it. The latter encompasses things like suggestion and reward systems, regular meetings where clearing the air is encouraged, and a formal system for getting the employee's input for areas that involve their work.

A common misconception is that good feedback and listening skills undermine your managerial authority. This simply isn't true, as you will see when you actually develop and use these skills. The buck stops with you as manager. You are empowered -- and paid -- to make the tough decisions in an organization. When you take steps to turn your employee relationships into a partnership among winners, respect for both you and your authority increases. There is a direct relationship between how important you make your staff feel and what degree of effort they'll put in for you.

There are two aspects to spending time with your staff. One is the extent to which they feel your door is open to talk to them. On one hand, you shouldn't encourage gratuitous interruptions, the more common problem is not being open enough. Examine how welcome people feel to come and talk to you; put it another way, what is your initial reaction to people when they come into your office? Do you welcome them, ignore them, or give in to a tendency to shoot the bearer of bad news? Ideally, you should have an open door, even with a busy schedule, and pair this with an open mind when your employees come in to speak with you. The other factor is the extent to which you actively solicit their feedback. Analyze the extent to which you go out of your way to spend time with them, listen to what their problems are, pat them on the back for the good things that they've done, and make them an important part of the team.

In order to make your employees feel important, you will have to make a conscious investment of time amidst other pressing matters during the workday. But it pays off handsomely. It becomes a self-fulfilling prophesy; when you treat them as part of a team, with important contributions to make, they become part of a team and make important contributions.

Particularly within a customer service environment, the people who work for you serve as your eyes and ears for how your customers feel, and how best to serve them. Management is not a democracy, since you will often be called upon to make decisions for the best interests of your group. Nevertheless, it's good policy and good business to make your employees part of the decision making process.

Actively solicit employee views as part of your normal information gathering process, and provide an open door for ongoing feedback. When your entire group of employees feels that they play an important role in the operations of your group, you not only tap into one of your most important sources of information, but take that critical step from being a group to being a team.

Marketing Yourself and Your Team

Likewise, it is just as important to keep your own management aware about what you've done, what problems you are having, and how to perform your job better. It follows that if you are the expert at what you do, management needs your feedback on the job. If you don't speak up, your good work may go unnoticed, your needs may not get addressed, and you might not get the help and advice to do an optimal job.

In an ideal world, customer service managers and their own upper management work together as a team to create excellent quality service. For many managers, however, the reality seem more like a constant struggle for adequate resources to do your job against people whose main job function appears to be constantly saying no. In these cases, here are some of the tools you will need.

Empathy for your management's agenda

There is a saying that "when you are a hammer, everything looks like a nail." In a similar manner, too many managers try to add resources and budgets for what they do, without paying enough attention to bottom-line costs and benefits for the whole organization. In today's lean environment, pressures to control costs continue to grow. Understanding these pressures help you work as a partner with your management. It's important to measure your needs against the company's bottom line, and seek creative ways to work together.

Good statistics

Customer service professionals know how important a reputation for excellent service is. With your management, however, you must be prepared to justify the bottom line impact of the need to improve these services.

One day, a magazine published a graph showing the high profitability of our company versus our nearest competitor. That graph, combined with our over 95% good-to-excellent ratings in customer surveys, became our team's legacy.

A later chapter will present some measurements you can use to assess service quality, including surveys, transaction records, and customer feedback.

Flexibility

The hallmark of a good service manager is the ability to look at options beyond throwing more people at a problem, such as cross-training, team approaches, and improvements in your service process. This, plus the flexibility to start small and demonstrate benefits to new approaches, will give you an edge over people who must always seek change in large and expensive leaps.

Good salesmanship

What your team is doing impacts the bottom line of your company, sometimes even more directly than its sales efforts. Learn to communicate ways in which your team's service efforts make an organization what it is, or what it could be.

Many people feel that they do communicate with their management and don't get results. A key question to ask yourself is: are you bringing your boss problems or solutions? If you simply dump problems, excuses and shortcomings in the lap of your supervisors, you won't be seen as someone who can be promoted to help solve these problems. The emphasis should always be on positive, constructive feedback. In addition, you score a lot more points for advice that is not purely self-serving but that improves the overall good of the organization.

I always had a rule with my own employees: never come to me with a problem unless you have at least one suggestion to fix it. I'd make exceptions for things like personal problems or what color to paint the office, but in general complaints and excuses were only OK if they were fruitful complaints and excuses. In a similar manner, you need to become a problem-solver and team player to succeed in working with your own management.

Keeping a Good Staff Motivated

Recently, a friend said, "I'll bet when you supervise people that work with the public, you've really got to lay down rules for how to deal with people and light a fire under them if they don't comply." The problem is that I suspect too many managers would nod their heads in agreement with this statement. That is perhaps one of the main reasons why the state of customer service is not always as good as it could be.

While high standards are quite important, by far the best way to maintain those high standards is to learn how to treat your employees like the valuable experts and professionals that they are. When you do, the odds are that they'll not only meet your high standards, but they'll use their own creativity and enthusiasm to raise those standards even higher. As a manager, your first and foremost task is to keep your customers happy. But never forget that developing your staff and motivating them to grow is a very close second.

Support everything you say with your own behavior and example. If you want your group to work on quality, don't be a manager who preaches quality once a year and production quotas twice a day. If you want cooperation with another group, don't make wisecracks and critical comments about them yourself. Because your employees generally want to please you, they will give you the behavior you seem to want – whether you like it or not.

Motivating people involves little more than treating people with respect and dignity, and expecting them to give their best on the job. Here are some ways to put this in practice include:

Provide regular doses of encouragement

Most people work for two kinds of compensation -- the paycheck they receive and respect and recognition for what they do. Perhaps the biggest difference that you can make as a leader is to actively notice the good things your employees do. Sometimes, there are tangible ways to express this. In his book *Managing to Have Fun*, consultant and psychologist Matt

Weinstein discusses how a national pharmacy chain would periodically distribute "scratch and win" prize cards for managers to pass out to their top performing employees[10]. Other times, simply noticing a job well done or a great attitude with co-workers can represent a very important and cost-free reward for people on your team.

While too much gratuitous praise – or, for that matter, criticism – won't have the desired effect, periodic encouragement and praise is the single best way to motivate people to higher levels of performance. This is true particularly in a field as tough as customer service, where no one can perform perfectly. If you read the biographies of successful people in fields ranging from sports to novel writing, you will find that many of them trace their success to some important figure in their life -- a teacher, a parent, a manager – who noticed their talents and cheered them on.

Keep your standards high

Treating employees well is in no way at cross purposes with expecting good performance from people. The distinction is one of coaching people to do well rather than bullying them to do so. Set high standards for yourself and everyone around you, and at the same time provide an environment where people can achieve these goals. Expecting great things from people can be a positive experience for everyone.

This means that when someone falls short, don't criticize them. Show them how to do the job better, and with courtesy and professionalism make it clear what your expectations are. With good employees who are capable of doing the job, these expectations will usually be met. With others who cannot or will not measure up -- well, that's why you're the manager, and you must ultimately maintain a team of quality people. In either case, never compromise your standards.

Reward quality, not just volume

Have you ever had the experience of repeatedly contacting a company's service center and receiving poor or inappropriate advice with each contact? Or have you been forced to go through an endless litany of voice menus seemingly designed to prevent you from ever reaching a knowledgeable person? In both cases, you are probably dealing with companies whose managers pay more attention to call statistics than customer satisfaction.

Remember that your employees will try to give you whatever you reward them for. It's all too easy for a beleaguered service manager to over-emphasize productivity and under-emphasize quality, with the end result being bad service. When it is clear that people are judged on how many transactions they process per hour, even the most customer-friendly people on your staff will start giving people short shrift to preserve your prized average transaction time. Instead, seek to reward overall customer satisfaction, and save your productivity concerns for people who vary far from the group's norms.

Don't overdo performance measurement

This automated age makes it easier than ever to determine exactly how many calls per hour an agent takes, how many items are checked per minute by supermarket checkers, even how many keystrokes are entered each second by a typist. On one hand, it's important to have knowledge of the personal productivity of each member of a group. On the other hand, an inexperienced or incompetent supervisor may find it too easy to cross the line between motivating good workers and making them feel like caged animals in a zoo. If you monitor people, be sure to look for overall good performance, and don't nit-pick at small deviations from the norm.

Give everyone a role in the operation

It is important to seek the expertise of your own front-line people at all levels of the team. Doing so will pay substantial dividends in long-term job satisfaction and productivity. When important decisions need to be made about work within the team, one of the most important phrases in your vocabulary should be "What do you think?"

> Recently, I toured a snack food plant with a group of managers. Our tour guide, a young line supervisor, told us of an episode one day when a problem was discovered in their potato chip processing line. A meeting was quickly convened by company management, whose key role was to listen to recommendations from a group of packers and line workers. In the end, they decided to destroy two shifts worth of potato chip production, totaling tens of thousands of cases of product, rather than risk the product's quality. Management backed their decision all of the way. While the company lost $40,000 worth of production that day, everyone involved felt that they preserved something much more valuable – their product's reputation.

Beyond protecting their customers, this company's management did something even more important for their own people: it let their own front line people take the lead role in a difficult decision, and thereby reaffirmed their importance to the company.

Most of all, motivating people gets to the basics of setting high (but attainable) standards, then encouraging and rewarding people to meet these standards -- and more importantly, making your employees an integral part of the process of providing good service. I subscribe to the view that people are basically good, and that most genuinely try to meet the wishes of the people responsible for their paychecks. When you set customer-oriented goals, and at the same time create a working environment that stands behind your employees and their best efforts, the result is generally both high performance and a good working environment.

Preventing Burnout

In the opening scene of the movie *Conan the Barbarian*, young Conan is led off as part of a horde of conquered children, and put to work chained to a treadmill. The film then fades to many years later, with a strapping, muscular Conan still chained to the same treadmill. This introduction is meant as an explanation for the two film hours of carnage that follow when he is finally unchained and proceeds to act like, well, a barbarian. Conan's antagonists might have literally kept their heads better had his employers learned a thing or two about preventing employee burnout.[11]

The modern equivalent of this scene might be one in which managers push their employees in front of the public with little team support or sense of purpose, criticize their every mistake, and leave them out there until they burn out and turn into Conan the Service Technician. With an enlightened view of one's employees and the working environment, however, this need not be the case.

Some people feel that burnout (an overload of stress and fatigue) is an occupational hazard of customer service, the same way that pro football can lead to concussions. I personally feel that it is perfectly possible to have a lengthy career in customer service without burning out, by following sound stress and time management principles. At the same time, one must recognize its potential in this intense, fast-paced profession, and take steps to prevent it. There are several steps you can take at an organizational level to prevent burnout.

Practice preventative medicine

Perhaps the most fundamental step that you can take to prevent burnout is providing a good working environment where people look forward to coming to work. If you set positive goals, are a good listener, keep everyone's workload appropriate to their resources, and back them up all the way, you are likely to see much less burnout -- and much better service -- in your group.

Watch the workload

It may sound naive in today's fast-paced environment to not overload the capacity of your staff. At the same time, when you look at the bottom line impact of chronic overwork, in terms of turnover, morale, stress levels, and above all service quality, you will find that this makes good business sense.

This is particularly true in customer service. A dispirited group of assembly line workers might conceivably be able to tighten more bolts if pressured to, but an overstressed customer service staff will always provide lower quality service. As employees see their workload increase beyond a reasonable level, customers start experiencing more curt transactions, increased buck-passing, and a general sense that everyone is more than happy to not help them. The wrong emphasis on productivity continues to ruin the reputations of a great many service organizations.

"Easy for him to say", you may think. "My group gets 500 calls per day, and my management won't budget money for more staff. There's no way that I can cut down on anyone's workload." Well, then, what would you do if your call load increased to 2000 calls per day, and they still didn't increase your budget? Would you tell everyone to work until they roll over and die? The truth is, as a manager you must often take the difficult step of making business decisions based on realistic workloads, and then seek other options from there. In this case, perhaps, you might look for ways to reduce the call volume through product improvements, phone system automation, improved productivity, a stronger case to management for realistic staffing levels, or in the worst case, even having more people wait on hold. In any case, the cornerstone of a quality service business must be realistic demands upon your employees.

Try putting the eight-hour day among your management objectives, and you will appreciate the results. This is one area where I personally have always practiced what I preach.

> Over the past twenty years, I've served as a manager during some of the hottest growth years of my employers in the software industry. Even in this environment, with never-ending change and competitive pressures, I have never once asked a single employee to work overtime. Believe it or not, we always met deadlines, achieved goals, and provided award-winning service.

Rotate duties

If people are delighted to do what they are doing for eight straight hours a day, that's great. Don't change a thing. But if people seem to be bored with repetitive tasks, consider putting one or more of these tasks on a rotational basis among a number of people.

Bear in mind here that everyone is different. I could spend weeks on end dealing live with customers, and can't stand repetitive paperwork. Other people are just the opposite. Look for creative ways to bring out the best in each person and do not let anyone get burned out doing the same thing over and over.

Celebrate milestones

Would you give your best year after year if you worked in a vacuum where nobody ever utters a compliment? You should, without overdoing it, keep an eye towards both recognizing group successes and individual achievements. Well timed awards and celebrations not only send a signal to team members that they are important, but helps reinforce the good performance that brought on the recognition.

Encourage professional development

Motivate people with professional opportunities appropriate to your business. Above all, promote customer service within your organization as a profession rather than just a job. Let your people develop as spokespersons within your organization, and within the industry, and perhaps even encourage people to write articles and take on speaking engagements. Use your group's valuable link to the customer as a connection to the other areas of the company, such as product development, education, training.

Restructure the work

There are creative ways to reduce burnout by using the resources of your whole team. For example, let's say that you run a telephone service center, everyone takes calls from anyone, and your staff are frustrated because they get interrupted too much to solve many of the problems generated by these calls. Try training some people to become experts in specific areas, and have them handle most calls in these areas. You may find that you can suddenly handle a greater workload with much less frustration.

Always keep the emphasis on increasing the organization's productivity while restructuring the workload. You are not just getting your group out of doing work, or shifting it off to someone else who must then work twice as hard. Striving for positive, constructive change to restructure the workload so that everybody is happy is the way to get the overall job done better, not to mention score points with your own management as a problem solver.

It must be stressed that burnout is rarely terminal or permanent. It is often a state that normal, healthy, talented people go through when they are chronically overloaded, or not getting adequate recognition for what they do. It can appear for reasons that are professional, personal or both. A workload and a level of intensity which doesn't bother people under normal circumstances may become a problem under a high state of personal stress. In either case, the best action is to recognize the signs of burnout and do something about it in the early stages, without letting either a job or a personal situation get out of hand.

Dealing with Problem Employees

No matter how well you tend to the needs of your employees, however, people will still bring their own unique personalities to the job. As a manager, you face the complex task of working with all of them. Positive, enthusiastic employees who contribute critical skills are easy to manage. Negative, difficult employees who don't contribute much are easy to manage as well – they usually get shown the door. One of the most common interpersonal challenges managers face is supervising people who are a mixture of good traits and bad ones.

You probably know many of these types already. They handle customers with aplomb, but are competitive and uncooperative with other team members. They are excellent team players, but have problems with their attendance. Or they are impatient about sharing their knowledge with others. Perhaps worst of all, they may create a bad experience for some of your customers.

In a customer service environment, these kinds of employees present a particular challenge, because your "product" demands good customer skills and team morale. Here are some guidelines for working with some of your more challenging staff:

- Make your performance expectations clear in terms of both job performance and team morale. Use work reviews, professional development, and counseling to get your message across. NEC's Ellen Dudley observes that, "Some people will ask why they haven't received a promotion -- and then I can leverage that dissatisfaction to point out what they would need to do to become promotable. In some cases, this has really turned around people who were once marginal into some of our more valuable employees."

- Use the "sandwich" approach in coaching employees about problems. Point out their good traits, then tell them what you feel is lacking, and end up by expressing confidence in the employee. By wrapping your concerns within a sandwich of praise and encouragement, you help give people hope and motivation to improve.

- Your constructive criticism is often met with a list of grievances on the part of the employee. Hear out whatever is bothering them, and separate legitimate grievances from posturing and personality. Then frankly acknowledge their concerns, while firmly keeping the focus on the employee's need to improve.
- Notice and encourage small changes in behavior. When recognized and praised, small steps in the right direction can lead to lasting improvement.
- See if a change of duties is warranted. Sometimes a bad attitude overlies deeper job dissatisfaction, such as a dislike for working with the public. Some people become remarkably better team members when moved into positions which better suit their temperament.
- Don't let chronically negative people work with the public.

Perhaps the toughest decisions you have to make as a manager involve people who are unable to meet your team's standards, no matter how much you coach or counsel them. Terminating someone is a decision that involves someone's livelihood and is increasingly fraught with legal ramifications today. And as one customer service manager puts it, "it never gets easier, no matter how many times you go through the process." When people are unable to perform up to expectations -- whether it involves customer skills, relationships with co-workers, absenteeism, or other problems -- there is both an ethical duty and a legal requirement to try and remedy the problems first, unless gross misconduct is involved. While a full discussion of the issues behind employee termination is beyond the scope of this book, here are some general guidelines.

- Work closely with your human resources department in any disciplinary matter.

- Focus on behaviors and not people.
- Follow a progressive discipline approach, starting with oral warnings and advancing to written reprimands, where it is made clear to the employee what steps are required to maintain their employment.
- Document all meetings and discussions with problem employees, including a dated record of items discussed and actions taken.
- Handle the actual termination as gently and humanely as the situation allows. Discuss your decision in terms of the fit between the job and the individual rather than as a case of failure, and let him or her leave with as much dignity as possible.

As a leader, you have to balance each employee's development against the quality of your group's services. It is important not to give up too quickly on people. Give them the feedback and coaching they need to meet your expectations. At the same time, your primary responsibility is to your organization and its customers; therefore you must ultimately insist that difficult employees channel their talents to the good of both your customers and your team's morale.

Looking Out For Your Team

Perhaps the single defining factor in the long term success of a customer service organization is whether its team members view it as a long term career. As a manager, you need to look out for the interests of your employees, both by your own policies, and your own efforts to sell a quality service organization to your own management. Here are some particular areas requiring attention.

- Delineate a clear career path, and an adequate reward structure for what your employees do. If your organization views customer service as the place to stick people who are too young or don't fit in elsewhere, it will often get what it deserves. Challenge this by seeking ways to reward and promote your top people with recognition equity such as position titles, responsibilities, and incentive awards. Provide them with opportunities to have a greater voice within the organization.
- Assure that your salary structure is competitive. Call up ten companies for service and you will be able to tell which ones pays their staff the least. It's a wise move to pay realistic wages and bonuses, and then make your staff part of a team effort to cut costs elsewhere.
- Develop an attitude that your group is the best group in the company, and get that message across to the rest of the organization.
- Learn to set goals instead of rules, where possible, and take a lead role in keeping petty regulations and policies to a minimum.

People do their best when they feel valued and trusted. Some firms make it clear that people may go beyond normal company policy when they feel it is in the best interests of their customers. Other firms even reward employees for bending the rules when it's the right thing to do. When you emphasize trust and professionalism instead of rules, regulations and discipline, your team is much more likely to work with you for the good of the organization.

Many of these issues depend upon your upper management's view of customer service, and its value to the organization. This makes it important for managers to track the effectiveness of their group, using tools such as customer surveys and transaction statistics, to make a persuasive case for the role of an excellent customer service operation. Customer service managers who can think like executives, and cost-justify the bottom line effects of providing great service, stand a better chance to obtain the resources they need to build a strong customer service environment.

Even within the worst of budgetary constraints, you can implement many important aspects of creating a professional customer service environment cost you nothing. These include:

- Giving everyone on your team authority and latitude to solve problems.
- Providing visibility for people to the rest of the organization.
- Recognizing your best people.

Most of all, take pride in the importance of both your own work and that of your team, and you will find that it's much easier to pull together to create great service.

Clone Yourself

Someone who has just asked their spouse to mow the lawn on a beautiful summer weekend might conclude that the human race avoids work whenever possible. In the ranks of management, however, many people have the opposite problem. They fail to delegate. It is one of the chief reasons that managers fail.

Delegating work to other people brings out some of our best and worst traits at the same time.

On one hand, it is easy to see the positives:

- You know you could work more efficiently with help.
- You want your staff to learn new things and grow.
- You want to be more effective as a team.

But on the other hand, the negatives may loom even larger:

- It takes time to train someone else, so you are tempted to put off tomorrow's productivity to get more done today.
- Pride (or, if you will, ego) says that no one can do the job as well as you can.
- You are reluctant to give other people more work.

Nevertheless, many managers are surprised at the good reaction they get from employees when they delegate meaningful tasks to them. As long as it is kept within reasonable bounds, most people like the feeling of being singled out for more responsibility because they are good at what they do.

The key to successful delegation lies in balancing more work with greater responsibility. In addition to delegating detail work that you don't have time for, if you also parcel out tasks that groom people for bigger things, the results are generally positive.

There's another, more subtle point to consider here as well. Your own promotability often depends in part on grooming people to carry on your current work. Learning to delegate as a win-win situation is perhaps one of the most important traits to cultivate as you and your organization grow over time.

Hire for Skills and Attitude

At Southwest Airlines, large numbers of potential employment candidates are brought together as a group, where each candidate is brought up in front of the group and asked questions. What many of the people in the audience don't realize, however, is that they are the ones being observed. Southwest personnel look to see who is paying attention and who is ignoring the proceedings, as a litmus test for how they might respond to customers.[12]

In the urgent, critical role of coordinating phone system repairs, NEC Business Communication Systems teams up with local temporary employment agencies to try out promising customer service center employees to make sure that they can treat customers well.

Both cases give a glimpse of how companies who take great service seriously take their hiring practices just as seriously.

One of the biggest parts of the management process is finding good people for your team. In fact, at upper levels of management in major industries, some executives spend as much as half of their time recruiting fellow executives. Hiring is a major responsibility because you generally have to work and build a relationship with whomever you bring aboard. Moreover, everyone brings with them both good and bad points, not all of which are apparent in an interview situation.

Like management in general, hiring people is a broad area of expertise unto itself, with many resources that can be consulted. The intention here is to bring out a few additional pointers to consider when you hire staff that work with the public.

Discussed earlier in the book was that customer service encompasses much more than a matter of attitude. At the same time, as a hiring criterion for people that work with customers, one's basic attitude towards others ranks far above most other job qualifications. Certainly, one must have enough intelligence and raw skills to perform the job. It is important to be able to work hard and think on one's feet. But, of greatest importance is a person's interpersonal skills – how a person interacts with the public and with peers, co-workers and management.

If you listed the five most important factors in hiring someone, attitude is factor one, two and three. No amount of expertise or skill in your field can make up for a poor attitude towards people, whereas people with a good attitude are often adaptable to learning the new skills of a given job. People with the right attitude are often much more productive than people with better qualifications on paper.

How can you evaluate a potential employee when you know everyone naturally puts their best foot forward in an interview? These tips have worked for many.

Trust your gut feelings

Your first impressions of a candidate often have more validity than you give them credit for.

Make the candidate feel good

A supportive interview environment both helps a candidate be frank in their responses, and provides a positive start to a future working relationship.

Get a feel for the learning curve

One of the most critical skills for a customer service professional is the ability to think on their feet. Provide time during the interview for some hands-on use of your product or service, or consider formal testing as another measure of basic skills.

Get your team involved

The candidate's chemistry with your team is every bit as important as their basic skills. Moreover, the opinions of the team can provide important feedback in making a hiring decision.

Check references

While understanding that references tend to be on the positive side, you should check out how the candidate performed in past positions. Look between the lines for signs of faint praise or possible unstated problems. A good candidate should have very strong, positive references from previous employers and colleagues.

The evaluation process becomes even more important when you are seeking to hire someone who will be a team supervisor or manager; for example, when a growing team lacks the experience for promotion from within. In addition to the issues mentioned above, one of the most critical points to evaluate is how well the candidate understands the nuts and bolts of what he or she will be supervising.

In the case of both team members and new managers, the people you recruit will have a direct impact on the nature of your customer service operation. Seek people who combine the skills you need with good personal chemistry, and ability to grow and change with the job. In time, good hiring skills will help you develop a team whose own group personality complements your own, and will continue the process of building this team into the future.

Developing Customer Service as a Profession

In many environments, front-line customer service is seen as the classic entry-level job where you leave people on the phones or behind the counter, plan for high turnover, and view them as the complaint department. There is a better way, however. With the right approach, customer service can become a respected path of employment within your organization, and a viable long-term career for your team members. Turning customer service from a job into a profession is perhaps the most important factor in retaining a strong, highly motivated team of people to work with your customers.

Unfortunately, some managers have trouble equating the terms *customer service* and *profession*. They may think, "What do you want me to do? Go out and raise everyone's salaries? I've got a business to run here." The problem here is missing the connection between cost and value. When you focus on increasing the value of people to your organization, it becomes easier in the long run to balance the cost of your team's efforts against its benefits. Many of the world's best service-driven organizations do, in fact, pay a premium for their employees. The benefits they generate, however, in terms of productivity, customer retention and market share tend to far outweigh any modest differences in salaries. So for many organizations, the first step is to examine the overall value of each person on their staff, then use professional development programs as a tool to increase that value.

Depending upon your particular environment, some of the tools that your organization might employ to promote professional development include:

Skills training

Teaching people new job-related skills is important from both a performance and a motivational standpoint. It requires an investment of both time and capital, but when the right skills are targeted, appropriate training programs should yield a measurable return on the investment. Depending upon your specific needs and budget, your options may range from training materials or videos, to programs taught by your own management or team members, all the way to on-site or off-site programs using professional trainers.

Continuing education

Encouraging people to pursue their own studies off-hours helps leverage your investment with their commitment of time, and can help people grow both personally and professionally. Many people have completed degree programs after hours, with the help and encouragement of their employer. Others may study targeted subject areas one course at a time. In turn, these programs often allow people to take on greater responsibilities at work and to build a commitment to the organization.

Certification

There are two main kinds of certification. Internal certification programs establish competency for defined roles within the organization. External certification programs provide professional licenses and certificates. You can use these programs to help assess the skill levels within your group, and help people set goals for themselves. Increasingly, such programs also provide documentation to help your organization meet formal quality standards or service quality benchmarks.

Professional activities

Many fields have professional societies or organizations. Encouraging people to be active in these groups helps them to develop leadership skills as well as keep in contact with other professionals in the field. In addition to work-related groups, other organizations such as Toastmasters International and Rotary may help people develop skills such as public speaking or leadership. Your support of these activities may range from simply providing facilities for meetings all the way to supplying employees with time off or financial support to participate in events.

Publishing and speaking opportunities

Encouraging people who like to write and speak is an excellent, low-cost employee development tool. Publishing opportunities include channels such as in-house publications, newsletters, trade press and national magazines, while speaking opportunities may include internal audiences, community groups or the aforementioned professional organizations. You can help support these activities by using the services of your internal marketing or public relations department to help place articles, or to provide speaking opportunities through your firm's meetings and conference activities. You might offer incentives such as publication awards for people who successfully get articles into print.

Leadership opportunities

It benefits both your company and your employees when you seek opportunities for people to perform beyond their customer service roles, even as they maintain their current jobs. Responsibilities such as teaching, consulting or internal advisory roles can leverage the experience your team members have working with your customer base, to help develop them as the corporate voice of the customer. Beyond helping the company, these assignments can help team members build their own sense of importance, and encourage them to take on greater roles within both the company and the profession.

Internal promotional opportunities
In seeking talent, many firms often miss out on developing a resource that is right under their noses – their own employees. By actively training and mentoring people throughout the life cycle of their careers, you can develop a strong pool of talent in advance of future needs.

Employee development requires a tangible effort on the part of a company to facilitate individual success, including promoting opportunities within the organization. An enlightened approach to internal career planning not only keeps top performers within the organization, but can help attract more talented people in the first place. Moreover, it puts greater responsibilities in the hands of people who already have a high level of buy-in to your service culture. This kind of investment in career development is generally a win-win situation for both the organization and the employee.

Many of these approaches represent high-payoff activities that can be put to work immediately and cost little or nothing to implement. Others have ongoing benefits which offset the modest cost involved. Both should be viewed as long-term investments. With turnover and retraining costs often running several thousands of dollars per employee, there is often a measurable, substantive return on the right kinds of employee development efforts.

Beyond formal employee development, one of the most important aspects of making customer service a profession is how your service professionals are viewed and rewarded within the company.

I will never forget my own first day at work after being promoted to become my company's director of customer services. My first task was to meet with upper management about where our group would be located as the company moved to a new building. The CFO's initial statement was, "Since your group is one of the back-office support functions of our company, we were planning to put you somewhere in the rear of the building."

I immediately responded with statistics about how our unusually high service ratings had helped fuel the company's 100 percent growth rate over the past year and how strongly I felt about promoting customer support as one of the most important functions in the firm. By the time I stepped off of my soapbox, our group was given prime window office space in the front of the building, with our own conference room!

You can take similar pride in what a respected, high-quality service team can accomplish within your own work environment. Never stop promoting its benefits to the rest of the organization.

Keep Your Eye on the Big Picture

Amidst all of the various challenges of being a customer service manager – customers, employees, management, and the organization -- one responsibility stands out. That responsibility is to look at the larger issues behind your group's role in the organization and the industry, and then set out to be the best in your field. From 24-hour service hotlines to providing eyeglasses in about an hour, nearly every major service-driven success story in today's industry began with managers who had the vision to do something better than anyone else had ever done it.

When former lumberjack Bill Boeing decided to build airplanes in 1916, he assembled a small team of people including carpenters, cabinetmakers and seamstresses to put his planes together in an old boathouse. Undoubtedly there were growth problems in those early days. But do not think that today's giant Boeing Company would be rolling out dozens of 747 jumbo jets if they had become overwhelmed by the supply and service problems of 1916.

For them and for you, one of the best ways to keep today's problems in perspective is to set your sights much higher. In your own job, keep an eye on where you want your growth to take you. Don't be the manager who grumbles about how bad the workload is getting – be the manager who's proud to expand and improve your services. Whether it's building a regional, national or worldwide network or going to 24-hour full time service or simply adding another staff member, a bigger workload should be managed so that it is a source of pride and success for you.

Don't be afraid to think big. It's better to fail at planning to succeed than to succeed at planning to fail. When you take a hard look at where you want to be next month, next year, and five years from now, you get your creative juices going on how to meet your goals. Once you set goals for growth, do more than think about it. Look into the nuts and bolts of how to meet those goals. Find out what's involved in setting up that toll-free hotline, or opening that regional center, or setting up that information booth in your store, and have your alternatives in place when the right time comes.

In today's highly competitive environment, the best customer service managers do more than supervise people or solve problems -- they serve as catalysts for change. This means observing both your team and the industry, then making customer service part of the feedback loop to improve your products and services. Such a global perspective makes you an important member of your organization, while taking nothing away from your primary mission as a manager: leading a team of people to create great service for each and every customer.

Step 5:

Learn How to Execute

_____

A few years ago, I watched a television interview where a well-known NFL football player discussed what factors led his team to the Super Bowl. I expected to hear comments about slamming quarterbacks to the ground and making linemen eat dirt. Instead, what followed sounded more like a math lecture. He discussed things like reading opposing offenses, signaling teammates, and following well-rehearsed routes where they might take two steps to the left, three steps forward, engage the tight end – and then finally slam the quarterback into the ground.

Finally, he looked into the camera and said, "We didn't get to the Super Bowl just because we have good people. Lots of teams have good people. We know how to execute better than most teams, and we execute very well."

What is true for football is equally true for customer service. If you take a randomly selected group of the nicest people you can find, throw them in a room, and call them a company, that alone will not produce good service. If you teach them a process that anticipates your customers' needs and how to react to them – in short, if they learn how to execute – then you will have good service. And when organizations learn to execute well, they learn the key to producing truly world-class service.

Executing well doesn't come naturally

This week, as I write this, I needed repairs on a lawnmower purchased long ago from a major national chain store. Before I took it in, I simply wanted to know how long the repairs would take. (My neighbors get a little touchy when there's a foot-high lawn next door.) First, I checked the local telephone directory for this store, and found a listing for lawn and garden repairs that directed me to an 800 number. I called it, and the conversation went as follows.

> **Me**: I need to get a new blade for my lawnmower, and would like to find out how long it would take to get that done.
> **Them**: Sir, you'll have to take the lawnmower to the store yourself.
> **Me**: That's fine, but could I speak to their repair department to see how long the repair would take?
> **Them**: You'd have to speak with them directly.
> **Me**: Would you have their phone number?
> **Them**: Those numbers are not listed, sir.

So I went back to the phone book, found the main number for the store, called them, and asked for lawn and garden repair. The person I was connected to told me that I would have to call yet another number to speak to the repair department. I dutifully hung up, called this next number, and after a few rings was greeted by the loud "Fweeee!" of a fax machine. Finally, I called the main number of the store again, and had the following discussion.

> **Me**: Hello. I tried to contact your repair department, and was connected to a fax machine.
> **Them**: They must be out. When they don't answer their phone, it connects to their fax machine.
> **Me**: So what should I do to reach them?
> **Them**: You'll have to try calling again when they're in.

Eventually, I ended up heaving the mower in my car trunk and going up there in person to see how long it would take to fix it.

To me, situations like the one above represent the great, hidden secret of customer service. These people didn't need a course in courtesy or how to handle difficult customers – everyone was polite if not terribly helpful, and I wasn't acting difficult. But did I receive a good service experience? And more importantly, where will I buy my next mower? The main reason that I did not come away happy is that I dealt with a group of individuals, and not with a system that made them a team.

Looking at these and other experiences, I firmly believe that knowing how to execute is the key difference between nice people and great service. Doing it well is not an innate part of human nature. It takes work, and is part of a lifelong learning process. In my mind, there are three components of executing well in customer service:

- Get your signals straight
- Measure the right things
- Be your own customer

These three steps are important tools to bridge the gap between what you provide and what your customers expect. Each of them requires the development of a process, whether you are a one-man consulting firm or a Fortune 500 company. Most importantly, when they are done well, they give you a substantial advantage in service quality over competitors who don't execute as well. Let's take a look at each of these factors in detail.

Get your signals straight

Let's say that a typical customer has 100 interactions with your company, and only one of those interactions is unpleasant. Guess which one will form their impression of you? How each person is trained to respond, and how these people work together with each other, makes the difference between a consistent excellent service experience and missing with "99 per cent." This makes it imperative that everyone works in harmony to meet the customer's needs, within a system that insures a good experience every time.

When companies develop a legendary service reputation, it usually isn't just because of individual heroics. There is always a system behind the service. Here are a few examples:

- At the Ritz-Carlton hotel chain, the company's core service quality standards are carried by each employee on a laminated card – and reinforced at daily departmental meetings, along with three full weeks of training per year. Even among the top tier of hotel properties, Ritz-Carlton has a legendary reputation for the level of personalized attention they provide their guests. For example, if you request a softer pillow at one hotel in California, their extensive guest database assures that one will be waiting for you in the future at any of their hotels worldwide.

- Every time a package changes hands at FedEx, a bar code on the package is scanned. At any time of day or night, customers can call FedEx's service center, or log on to their web page, and see exactly where their parcel is among the millions of packages they ship each day.

- At Joe's Restaurant, you are greeted and have your drink order taken within 30 seconds of being seated at your table. A computerized system makes sure your meal gets to the right place quickly as it goes from the kitchen, to specific locations on trays picked up by the waitstaff, to numbered chair locations at your table. A manager is on the floor at all times quietly tracking how you are being greeted and served, how quickly your check and change are processed, and how the operation is going overall.

In each of these cases, these companies thought beyond the usual process of treating people well, and into how to effectively deploy the resources of a team. More importantly, each person knows their own role, and how they interact with the other members of the team.

Above all, having a system for good service moves your organization beyond human nature, and into an environment where you can plan to deliver world-class service. By setting clear goals and procedures, your service quality becomes a matter of execution rather than mood. Here are some of the key factors in getting your own team's signals straight.

Develop a process

Many employers teach their employees job skills, such as how to operate a cash register, how to issue a boarding pass, or how to make an ice cream sundae. The best service-driven companies go beyond this, and teach people how to be part of the process that a typical customer goes through. For example, instead of just running a cash register, they may learn how to process an order, answer common product questions, work together with your team when someone needs a price check, and perhaps do some suggestive selling or discounting. Teaching the right process often makes all the difference between being a customer's advocate and "I just work here."

These guidelines form an important part of your organization's overall identity to the customer, as well as how to deliver a consistent service experience from person to person. This sense of who we are then becomes part of your culture. For example, mail-order clothing giant Lands' End is famous for training its call center employees to answer nearly any question about their thousands of products right on the phone, as well as keep track of each customer has ordered in the past. This leads to a very consultative ordering environment that has made it easier for consumers to accept the once-unthinkable practice of ordering clothing by telephone.

Manage the exceptions

Teach everyone on your service team what to do in common situations that go outside your process. These include details such as whom to contact, limits on what can and cannot be done, and how your organization likes to resolve these situations. This can range from how and when to contact a manager, to what to do in an emergency. More importantly, make it clear what the preferred response is in situations that are outside the bounds of a normal transaction. For example, one store manager in the Wegmans supermarket chain has a delightful rule that when employees plan to say "yes" to a customer, they may go ahead and do so, but if they plan to say "no" to a customer, they must first contact a manager.

Know when to escalate

Many customer problems are caused by a failure to escalate problems to the people best qualified to handle them. This is a particular problem in environments where employees feel that they "lose face" by not being able to take care of problems themselves – so they give you bad service rather than put your problem in the right hands. The common case where you call a technical support line for help, and you feel pushed off the phone with a poor answer, is a good example of a failure to escalate.

You solve this problem by setting clear guidelines for when to get other people involved, together with fostering an environment where getting the right problems to the right people is encouraged rather than punished. For example, as a help desk manager, I have always had three clear rules for handling technical support calls:

- If you can handle the problem yourself, keep the call.
- If you cannot handle the problem yourself, but could learn about how to solve it, set up a conference call with one of the experts on the team, and still keep the call.
- If you cannot handle the call yourself, and cannot learn productively how to solve it, escalate it to an expert.

Conversely, you need to make sure that escalation does not turn into customers being bounced indiscriminately from one person to another. One powerful technique you can use to avoid this is the "warm transfer," where representatives personally introduce the customer to the expert, discuss the problem, and formally transfer ownership of it. Combined with proper management oversight, using the warm transfer has the benefit of creating a team response for customers, and a learning opportunity for your team members, as well as removing the need for customers to explain their issues over and over again to new people.

Cross boundaries

A common thread across many world-class organizations is a clear shift from job responsibilities to global service responsibilities. Instead of having highly specialized people who feel that something is "not their job," they have a team of people committed to reaching service goals, and doing whatever is needed to make these goals happen.

> At Southwest Airlines, part of their process revolves around "turning around" an aircraft from arrival to departure within 15 minutes, a figure that is around twice as fast as many of their competitors. To achieve this goal, pilots will load bags on airplanes alongside the baggage handlers, flight attendants will help pick up the cabin, and ground crews will do whatever it takes to facilitate the needs of the flight crew. Similarly, 3M Corporation's Dental Products Division, a winner of the Malcolm Baldridge National Quality Award, succeeded in doubling its sales volume with minimal increase in head count by deploying its employees into over 150 cross-functional teams.

Whatever business you are in, very low boundaries between job functions is a core trait of today's market and service leaders.

Learn from experience

Service quality doesn't end with putting a strong process in place. Continue to look critically at what aspects of your process do and don't work for your customers, and then use that feedback to continually improve your operations.

The trends that you see while serving your customers can affect your business in both immediate and global terms. For example, seeing that customers at your bank spend too much time waiting in line might lead you to rearrange your lobby – but at another level, might also lead you to implement services such as on-line and telephone banking, and change your market model entirely. In both cases, using your customers as part of a lifelong learning process can become a key factor in your success in the marketplace.

Given the benefits of good service teamwork, why doesn't everyone manage people around a service process? Perhaps because it takes more work than simply teaching people the functions of their job. More importantly, on a day-to-day basis, it often means getting out of your comfort zone as a manager and coaching people to go beyond the narrow bounds of their job description. For those who do choose this path, however, these issues become a key part of their competitive advantage over other organizations.

Measure the right things

Do you know anyone who hates to balance their checkbook, and never sets a budget? When you just deposit your paycheck and then spend what you feel like spending, it can be easy to find there is "too much month at the end of the money." In the same way, you need to keep an eye on service metrics, so you can stay on track.

A regular review of your customer services provides a goldmine of information, for both you and the rest of the company.

- It tells you where to put your resources by identifying common problems.
- It points out areas where educating your customer better can reduce your workload.
- It can provide information to improve your products so they need less service and support in the future.
- It provides a means to greater profits by pointing out needs that might be filled by new products and services.
- Most importantly, it provides an overall pulse of your service quality.

Measuring your service performance is one of the best ways to develop world-class customer service. It can also be the quickest way to ruin your service reputation. Compare these two situations.

- You run a small restaurant, and you periodically greet customers as they leave and ask them a few short questions about how they liked their food and service. You use this feedback to make periodic changes in the menu, and develop a common training program across your entire front-line team. The restaurant's popularity soars as word spreads, and more and more people stop in to eat.
- You manage the customer support department of a medium-sized software firm, and surveys show that customers are frustrated by how long it takes to get through to people. In response, you create incentives based on how many calls

each representative handles per day. These numbers do go up, but it seems that customers are now more unhappy than ever: an increasing number claim that they are being rushed off the phone with poor quality answers. Recently, you've even discovered that some support representatives have been asking friends and relatives to call them repeatedly at work, to help them keep their "numbers" up and earn the incentives.

In the first case, you measured the most important thing – customer satisfaction – and then took strategic steps to increase it. In the second case, you put too much emphasis on a metric that actually hurt your service reputation. Measuring the right things, and creating the right policies in response, can have a major impact on both your service quality and ultimately your success in the marketplace.

The Basics of Keeping Track

One of the best aspects of using customer feedback for tracking purposes is that the information is either already there for the taking, or easily obtained. It then becomes a matter of tuning your procedures to capture this information and put it to good use. Here are some common ways that you can keep track of your organizational information.

Customer transaction records

If your primary interactions with customers take place when they come to you with problems -- for example, a service department or a help desk -- one of the basic ways to take your organization's pulse is to save and analyze records of what you do for customers.

These records can help make a direct impact on your bottom line by pointing out areas of improvement. Suppose that you manufacture certain kinds of machinery. If service records show that most customer complaints are on one particular kind of machine, you might use this feedback to improve its design. Likewise, if you discover repeated calls about how to use your equipment, you could increase customer satisfaction by improving your educational materials to address the most common questions. These contacts serve as valuable feedback, because they represent information from people who made the effort to contact you.

The best way to collect this information depends on your specific industry, your transaction volume, and the organization's overall style. With many kinds of customer transactions you can save and analyze the records that get regularly generated anyway. Other kinds of record keeping might be added painlessly to the process. And in this era of automation, it is increasingly common for front-line customer service personnel to log the results of their transactions within an on-line database, using tools such as help desk automation software or problem tracking systems.

At the same time, be aware of the limits of tracking customer transactions. Just as people in a hospital only represent a limited sample of people as a whole, customers who need service from you represent only a limited sample of your general customer base. These transactions, combined with information from your total customer base, however, can form an important part of the market research that should drive a service-oriented organization.

Customer feedback

A more broad-based form of information -- and a more accurate barometer of how your company is doing overall -- is feedback from a cross-section of all of your customers. Some of the ways of gathering this information include customer comment forms, or hotlines, and customer surveys.

Customer comments can be solicited in a number of ways. Comment cards or forms are often made available in public businesses such as hotels, stores and restaurants, while other firms include comment forms with their products or direct mail pieces. Other firms go as far as setting up and publicizing specific hotlines or electronic mail addresses for customer feedback. Contrary to popular belief, these mechanisms do not only attract responses from people who are unhappy. A surprising number of people will go out of their way to compliment good service experiences as well as complain about bad ones. Either way, these unsolicited comments serve as a good barometer of how you are doing.

Those customer surveys where you take action yourself to contact customers can take many forms. For a known customer base, a written or phone survey of people on your customer list gives a chance for customers to express their feelings about your products and services. Writing lets people be anonymous and, to some extent, more frank. On the other hand, calling people guarantees a high response rate and a better cross-section of opinion -- because generally, people with complaints are more motivated to respond to a written survey. Take your pick. For a more general customer base, a random survey of people who may or may not be customers of your firm may be more appropriate.

The kinds of feedback that you seek should be tailored to the nature of your business. For example, if you run a carnival, you don't want to hand every kid a survey as they step off the Ferris wheel. But twice a year, for example, you could hand a few customers a bunch of free tickets in return for some feedback. Some other guidelines for good survey etiquette are listed here.

- Respect your customer's time. Keep surveys short and focus their content on areas most of interest to your business.
- Beware of abusing these surveys as opportunities to make sales pitches. Such tactics turn people off and give legitimate customer surveys a bad name.
- To increase the response rate, consider providing people with a token of appreciation such as a free sample. Once, for example, a restaurant manager accosted me after dinner with a survey about my dining preferences, then gave me a coupon for a free ice cream cone. When I mentioned this to my wife, she wanted to go take the survey too!

Most importantly, be prepared to act as a result of your survey feedback. A survey not only tells you how well you are doing, but gives people a chance to get specific problems with your company off their chest. Tell them that you will investigate these problems, and then do it. You may never have a better chance to turn a malcontent into a lifelong customer than by giving their complaints first class treatment.

Employee feedback

Your employees are professionals, too, so don't leave them out of the process of designing a feedback system to record your effectiveness. They know your customers better than anyone. Moreover, a regular survey of your employees is a great way to find out, from the trenches, how your customers are doing. And if you are a manager, be sure to have an open door policy that encourages feedback the rest of the time as well. When people think of employee feedback, the first thing that often comes to mind is the traditional suggestion box. While there is a place for this, it is also important to be more proactive in bringing your employees into the process of improving your customer service. Some other approaches that are effective include:

- Provide recognition and financial rewards for employee initiatives that improve service or control costs.
- Give employees from all walks of the company the opportunity to be part of a formal advisory board. When used properly, such groups can be an active source of ideas for improvement. To keep this from becoming routine committee work, keep meetings short but active, choose participants who are motivated to improve rather than complain, and above all, listen and respond to their suggestions.
- Always consult employees first when considering changes that affect their duties. This is crucial both in obtaining employee buyoff on decisions, and looking at alternatives from the perspective of their expertise.

Bringing employees into the feedback process can be a good springboard for developing leadership skills and a sense of ownership. It's also an important part of making the best use of a company's most valuable resource. So long as employees feel that they are being listened to, and responded to, this kind of feedback helps to build a strong team relationship within a service organization.

Customer groups and advisory boards

Many customers consider it an honor to be asked to help companies improve their products and services; Ford Motor Company, as one example, once ran full page advertisements about how they invited people from all walks of life to Ford to discuss their preferences with the company. As a manager, I once helped set up a group of customers and sales representatives who were brought in regularly to advise our company on how best to redesign the user interface to our software. As users of the product, they had a perspective that we would have never had as product developers, and their suggestions played a strong role in the success of the new product.

To get direct feedback from customers as a group, businesses can either gather them together, or take advantage of situations where they are already gathered. For example, some companies will leverage their own conferences and seminars as a strategic opportunity to learn from their customers.

The CBORD Group, a company that develops foodservice automation systems, hosts an annual conference that is legendary among both its customers and the foodservice industry. Even in today's era of tight travel budgets, a surprising percentage of its customers make the trek to the company's Upstate New York headquarters every year from all over the United States, and many have been attending the weeklong event for a decade or more. Some customers liken it more to a family reunion than a convention.

Like many conferences, CBORD's User Group Conference has educational sessions on using its products, workshops on career and life skills, tours of the company, and evening social events. What is different is how much interaction is designed between customers and CBORD:

- Customer support representatives and other employees make it a point to meet customers they work with over the telephone during the year, and some representatives have even been known to take customers with special interests to places like craft fairs or shopping.
- Closed-door meetings are scheduled for customers, to which no company members are allowed. At the end of the conference, the company's senior executives respond frankly and directly to the issues that attendees have raised. These meetings are seen by CBORD as being the heart of the conference, and customers are encouraged to create prioritized lists that help drive its product development plans for the next year.
- Upon arrival, each person is given a "buddy card" that pairs him or her off with both a company employee and an experienced conference attendee. Buddies then compete for prizes by filling out information sheets on each other. Later in the conference, evening social events pit customers and employees in competitive events designed to get people to know each other well.
- Interactive kiosks with touch screens contain information about the conference, pictures and bios of company employees, and even a nutritional analysis of each of the meals being served.

Beyond its formal events, people at CBORD see the conference as a chance to put their legendary service culture into action in front of their customers. For example, one customer arrived with her two young sons – only to discover that her husband, who was going to meet her there and mind the children, couldn't make it at the last minute. A team of CBORD employees jumped into action to care for the children so the mother could attend the conference, arranging movies, a visit to one employee's home to play with her own children, and rides on the conference shuttle van.

Customers attend this conference to learn new things, and CBORD gains valuable strategic information from them in return. But there is a deeper benefit as well. By the end of the conference, customers leave as friends with several personal contacts at this 200-person company – and when competitive salespeople come calling, they often discover that these customers are reluctant to stop doing business with their friends.

As a service-driven organization becomes big enough, it makes sense to formally seek advice from its customer community through means such as users groups or advisory boards. Some ways to use these resources effectively are noted here.

- Keep the group independent from your company. It is OK to provide support, facilities or funding for the group, but your most important objective is to promote a free exchange of ideas from its participants.
- Obtain a good cross-section of opinions, and be careful of focusing on large customers: very often, the most important suggestions come from new users, prospects, sales distributors, and other channels. With the aforementioned example from my software firm, I found that longstanding customers were all too happy with an aging user interface, because they were used to it. It was newer customers who pushed us in the directions that the market wanted, and we

responded by designing the product to satisfy both old and new users.

- Seek members who are interested in constructively working with your company to improve its products and services. Frank feedback, including complaints, should be welcomed: the challenge in maintaining such a group is separating people with constructive criticism from the people who, by virtue of personality, are among the "professional bellyachers" to be found in any industry.
- Rotate people in and out of the group to maintain a fresh set of opinions, and prevent people from becoming too established as career committee members.

With these guidelines in mind, never forget that advisory work represents a major commitment of time for the participants. This means that this time should be respected, and kept to a minimum. It also means that the realities of staffing such a group often means that you will need to expend a certain amount of effort to keep it going, particularly with people who are committed to improving your organization. Nonetheless, once an organization reaches a certain size, such groups are an important means of getting close to your customers and their needs.

These techniques represent the basics of obtaining customer feedback and tracking information. There are, of course, many variations. For example, one company polls customers annually at its conference using an on-line survey and free t-shirts, while other customers are approached directly by research firms in venues such as shopping malls and baseball stadiums. Whatever mechanisms make sense for your company, it is important that your record keeping does not interfere with the smooth flow of work -- and above all, does not interfere with keeping customers happy! Have you ever heard the term *bureaucracy*? There are many places, inside and outside government, which do excellent record keeping but do not rate high on the list of customer satisfaction. Try to forge a happy medium between too much red tape and too little self-knowledge.

Plugging Into the Feedback Loop

Once information is gathered from customers, the next step is using it effectively within your organization. Those of us in the business of customer service have this fantasy that if we treat every customer well, people will flock to our company and make us all rich.

Unfortunately, if your company makes products that don't work, or isn't responsive to the needs of the market, your good intentions will sink with the rest of the ship. Making customers happy is just half of the job. At the management level, customer service must be an informational resource for the rest of the company as well. You are, after all, the only part of the company that deals regularly with its lifeblood, the customers.

Some of the ways you can convert your customer feedback into helping your organization become more profitable follow.

Improve your existing service levels

No one knows how to improve your company's customer service better than the people who work with your customers. They see what benefits the customers get and, more importantly, what problems and shortcomings the operation has. For example, you may know from your service experiences that people would prefer better documentation or your service hours as a convenience for people who work other shifts.

Customer service managers should make sure that there is a quick, easy mechanism for its service professionals to share suggestions and problems with the people who can do something about them. Moreover, there should be a regular process of review so that they can keep on top of how your customers' biggest problems are being addressed. Central to all of this is a positive, constructive relationship with the all parts of the service operation. People should be on guard against the "Hey, when are you guys going to fix this?" attitude, and instead work with people to focus their efforts.

Turn customer problems into sales leads

Sometimes, customers will share with you problems that additional products or services of yours could solve. This is an excellent opportunity for you or your sales staff to engage in consultative selling and make both parties happy by providing the needed solution.

Whether you are personally involved in sales or not, it is important to have an organized system to ensure that valuable leads are followed up. This could range from slips of paper and personal referrals, all the way to an on-line database. But make sure it is easy to generate a sales opportunity without adding too much work to the customer transaction. Just remember a couple of golden rules to keep the sales side of the customer equation from getting out of hand.

- Always do whatever you can to solve the customer's problem without any additional costs.
- Don't be so aggressively sales-oriented that people are afraid to come to you for help, and above all, never pressure customers. Have you ever bought your car in for an oil change, and received a sales pitch for how desperately you

need tires, a wheel alignment, and brakes? They may well be right, but timing and attitude are key. A blatantly obvious sales orientation turns people off and scares away repeat business.

See yourself as a consultant who is working to meet your customers needs, both for service from you, and perhaps additional products or services. When approached in terms of a win-win situation with your customer, service transactions that can and should lead to sales are an opportunity to generate good will on both sides.

Become part of the product development cycle

Your experiences with customers provide valuable raw data for what to do in the future. Thanks to your perspective, people in your company can learn that people would prefer your product to be shorter, or available in more colors, or more suited to left-handed users. More importantly, you can give people a sense of the mood of your overall customer base.

Offer your services as part of the initial design of new products to serve as the voice of the customer, either by providing raw information for people to use or, perhaps, by getting personally involved yourself. This is one of the areas where good customer service rises above being merely the complaint department and becomes an important profession within an organization. There are many facets to keeping customers happy. Some of them are short term, such as providing helpful advice and fixing problems. Others are longer term, such as taking an overall look at what your customers are telling you. Perhaps the biggest, overall measure of your success is how much your company improves what it gives the public.

When people would ask me what my long-term goals were in customer service, my standard answer would be to spend less time fighting short-term fires and more time contributing to the long-term professional growth of my organization. So do both your company and yourself a favor -- use your day-to-day efforts as building blocks to bigger and better things.

Information Equals Profits

In summary, it is important to realize that your customer contacts do not just represent isolated points in time. They are part of an overall process of sharing information in both directions, and this information is of great value to your organization when harnessed. If you are managing this feedback properly, your operation should be able to answers these key questions.

- How happy are your customers?
- Is your company listening to its customers? How can they contact you? How do their concerns get handled?
- What kind of visibility does your management have on the customer's needs, problems, and feelings about your product or service?
- What mechanisms are in place to track longer-term customer problems and trends?
- How does your company communicate with its customer base?

Understanding issues such as these is the first step towards a very interactive, productive relationship with your customers. When tracked and managed properly, these customer concerns represent opportunities to build long-term customer relationships, improve your competitive standing, and ultimately profit from the way that you treat your customers.

Be your own customer

Once in a while I see news reports about companies who are in trouble, and hear analysts discuss factors like their labor costs, their market share, or their debenture financing. I often smile when I hear these, because deep down inside I know that if these people would only eat at their own restaurants, fly on their own airline, or try to get a problem solved by their own service center, they would know why their company has a problem. They have lost touch with what it is like to be their own customer.

Thinking like a customer is much harder than it sounds, because human beings have a strong built-in tendency to shift perspective. When we are driving a car, we wish that those slowpoke pedestrians would get out of our way. Then when we are pedestrians, we wish that those cars would stop zooming by too close to us. No matter how much we think we know better, we shift effortlessly back and forth between perspectives like these every day. The same is true of customer service: when we are customers ourselves, we feel acutely where service could be better. But when we are the ones doing the serving, we suddenly see the world differently. We are tempted to see a customer as an interruption, as someone who didn't read the manual, as someone who doesn't understand company policy, or even as someone whose needs intimidate us.

This phenomenon is a big part of the reason customer service is not as good as it should be. It is also a reason why simply wagging your finger at an organization about delivering better customer service isn't effective. To really understand your own service quality and then take steps to improve it, you must have a process that lets people see your organization the same way that your customers do.

A simple case

Let's say that you wake up one morning and decide to start a company that makes widgets. You create an engineering department, and instruct them to design widgets as quickly and cost-effectively as possible. Then you create a sales department and tie their compensation to how many widgets they sell. Next, you build a shipping department and task them with shipping as many widgets as possible. You then hire a customer service department and tell them to keep your customers as happy as possible. Finally, you open the doors for business, and retreat to your corner office. Here's what will happen before long:

- One customer will complain that his widget doesn't work properly, a customer service representative will ask your engineering department to help look into the problem, and he will be told they are "too busy right now" – because they are behind schedule on your deadline to design the company's latest model widget.
- Another customer will turn out to be hopelessly incompetent in using the product, and the customer service rep will ask the sales department to do a better job of qualifying prospects in the future. Problem is, they are under pressure to meet this

month's sales quota, so they will mutter under their breath about the customer service team being the "sales prevention department" and take no action.

- Another customer calls just before closing time, and urgently needs a new widget shipped this evening. A voice mail is left for the shipping department with the customer's address and part number, but the next morning a return message is left – nothing can be shipped unless your lengthy shipping form is filled out in detail. After all, if the shipping department had to do this themselves, it would slow down how many packages they can ship per day.

In each of these cases, you have a situation where everyone is doing exactly what you asked them, but nobody is doing what you really want. And no amount of company rallies, mission statements or customer service slogans will ever change this. What will change things is setting policies that get everyone on your team to think like a customer.

In cases like the ones above, the important thing is not for a "customer service" department to win every battle. In fact, a company that does a good job of thinking like its customers should require less formal customer service, by anticipating their needs better. The real goal is to get your whole team on the same page to put quality products and services in front of your customers, set reasonable guidelines that balance service and productivity, and then meet customer needs as a unified whole.

Thinking like your customers

Thinking like a customer does take work, but the good news is that there are clear steps you can take to make it a habit within your own organization. Here are some of the ways that you can put the customer's perspective to work for you:

Do what the customer does

First and foremost, take every opportunity to use your products and services the same way your customers do, so you can understand their experience with your company at a gut level. If you can be a customer anonymously, all the better, but in either case do what you can to experience your company as the public does. Your intent should not be to "catch" people who don't measure up: the wrong (read: punitive) emphasis can backfire on morale and productivity. Instead, focus on gathering data that helps you coach people, and change policies, to improve your service operations.

> Sheetz, Inc., a Pennsylvania-based convenience store chain, implemented consistent service standards as a major part of the chain's resurgence to become one of the top 50 convenience stores in America. To back up these standards, its president would often travel personally by car to Sheetz stores, where a fellow employee would go into the store, purchase something, and see if the person behind the counter greeted him and handled the transaction properly. If he or she did, the president would then come in, shake their hand, and have a picture taken with him to publish in the corporate newsletter. These "surprise visits" went a long way to reinforce the company's focus on a consistent customer experience for everyone.[13]

Benchmark what your customers do

Beyond sharing your customer's experiences, use the data from them as a benchmark for your own operations: how long does it take to reach someone on the phone? How are they greeted?

How are difficult problems handled? These metrics put some structure to how your service quality compares with that of your competition.

Compare best practices

When one company provides an excellent service experience, it raises the bar for service standards in every business. This means that no business can afford to limit their attention to just the practices of their own market, particularly in today's global economy. Look critically at the best service practices that your customers experience in other industries, and see if there are lessons in them for your organization.

Get your management involved

In the widget company example above, you have an environment where the leader of each group is telling their team to meet the group's objectives, not the customer's (and the company's) objectives. Fixing this requires managers to work as a team on how balance customer needs with the needs of your company.

There is such a thing as too much service – or too much emphasis on production. When service demands consistently interfere with a company's ability to keep up with the market, or make a profit, the company will fail. At the same time, a more common problem is when an organization preaches customer service quality twice a year, and shipping products out the door five times a day. This too can kill a company. Only by getting your entire management team together in an ongoing, collaborative effort can you focus on driving world-class service within a profitable company.

Think multi-disciplinary

Seek opportunities to get people into the roles of other parts of your organization. These can range from joint meetings all the way to cross-functional training or "sabbaticals" in other departments. When people get a taste of what each department does, they do a better job of "owning" the agenda of each group and working as a team to benefit your customers.

More than anything, thinking like a customer needs to go beyond policies and procedures, and into the heart and soul of your business. When people on your team truly think like customers, they each become managers unto themselves: instead of passively waiting for "the boss" to tell them what to do, they take action based on what best serves the interests of your customers and your company. Backed up by a strong infrastructure for meeting customer needs, this philosophy is perhaps the key defining trait of delivering legendary customer service.

Your customers see more than customer service

There is a saying that the real function of a customer service team is to put itself out of business. The truth behind that statement is that world-class customer service is not just a function isolated to one department, but a culture that permeates the entire organization. Done well, it helps move a company from fixing problems to finding ways to satisfy needs better in the first place. Done consistently, it can have a dramatic impact on a company's market share and profitability.

The key to all of this is getting your whole team to execute properly, just like a championship pro football team. With the right process in place, good service becomes a choice, not just a chance. More importantly, this process can become a powerful tool for your own team's development. Deep down inside, most people want to be successful, and a clear game plan gives everyone on your team the opportunity to accomplish great things for themselves and your customers. In the next chapter, we'll discuss the "step" that puts these plans into action – building internal customer relationships within your team, and your organization.

Step 6:

Turn Your Whole Company Into the Customer Service Team

No matter how hard we work, most of us depend on the backup of an entire organization to satisfy our customers.

Early in her career, my wife worked the night shift at a doughnut shop. She was great with customers, and handled the counter duties with aplomb. Yet one evening, she had nearly every single customer angry with her. Why? Because the store manager fouled up that night and forgot to have any doughnuts delivered!

At their root, nearly all human relationships involve serving others. Within the customer service field, people often pay the most attention to serving their obvious customers, the ones who buy their product or service. A more subtle, but equally important part of your success is the relationship you build with the internal customers within your organization. If you look critically at each and every person's job within your organization, they all have "customers" in some shape or form -- perhaps as few people as their own manager, or as many as the entire firm. Understanding and managing these internal customer relationships for your own work in customer service, both among those you serve and those who serve you, is crucial to your ability to provide great service. Managed properly, they can turn your entire organization into a seamless customer service team.

Frank Gaines, an airline pilot for Southwest Airlines, underscores the importance of these relationships at his carrier. "Everyone rows in the same direction. One area where I immediately noticed it was in the relationship between the pilots and mechanics. Southwest fosters the idea of 'internal customers' and the pilots are the mechanics' customers. I know this sounds corny but it really works. The mechanics have a great attitude, do great work, and challenge themselves to get the job done with minimal delay to the aircraft's schedule."

As of this writing, Southwest has been a rarity within the airline industry, being a low-fare carrier with high profits, an excellent safety record, and high levels of customer satisfaction. Gaines makes a strong case that internal team relationships play a key role in this success. "It's like the attitude you'd like to have at your favorite service center for your car... good, quick, friendly service. At several of the maintenance bases the pilots sponsor and run a barbecue for the mechanics once a year.

Compared to my previous employers, it is utopia, and I feel much of the reason is due to the corporate culture at Southwest."

This chapter will present some of the key issues in working with your internal customers: identifying the proper relationships, building effective lines of communication, and most of all, understanding the dynamics of dealing with the people with whom you work day after day.

Understanding Your Internal Customer Relationships

As a consumer, you expect others to provide you with goods and services, from the local grocery store to the kid who mows your lawn. Your organization is no different: it is, ultimately, a network of people with needs and people who fill those needs. You can think of them as internal customers dealing with internal suppliers.

Within an organization, there are two basic kinds of internal customer relationships: direct relationships, where output is directly tied to needs, and support relationships, where you services are sought from others when needed. The former kind is perhaps like your newspaper carrier, where you control a commitment for their services. The latter kind, support relationships, are more like calling the fire department -- you can't plan when you need them, and they'll come if they aren't tied up on even more important calls.

Direct relationships are the most easily understood, and generally receive the most management attention. Support relationships, on the other hand, can be more difficult to manage because they often involve competition for the resources you don't have authority over. Moreover, these relationships are frequently the most critical ones for a customer service operation, involving people who provide the expertise to solve your more complex problems or backup resources during peak workloads.

The most important such support relationships often revolve around groups who provide the expertise or authority to resolve customer problems which go beyond your own team's front lines. A customer service team often has its own internal customers as well. For example, it may be responsible for supplying needed customer information for product planning and trends, or for taking customer data and turning it into sales leads. Above all, it serves the organization as a whole by functioning as its interface to their customers.

Unfortunately, groups that depend upon each other for support can also get in each other's way. Take, for example, one firm's sales and customer service departments. These two departments sometimes make work for one another and have the potential to frustrate each other in the process. Listen to some recent complaints from this company's top salesperson and their customer service manager.

Salesperson: One of my long time clients had a problem with their product, and some rude slob in customer service told them it must have been their fault. I talked to his manager about it, and he went into a long diatribe about how customers should be trained better. I just got word yesterday that the client is now talking with our competitors.

Customer service manager: These people in the sales department are selling a complex product to anyone who walks in off the street, and then leaving it up to us to deal with all of these poorly-trained users after the sale. It seems that nowadays, the main criterion for qualifying a sales prospect is that they have a pulse. Ever since the company set a goal to increase sales by 20 per cent, our customer service volume has doubled.

So who is right here? Neither of them, and both of them. A situation like this shows each group talking past the other and not paying any attention to the agenda of the other. In addition, both groups view the other as making it difficult for them to satisfy their own management. More importantly, frustrations have grown to the point where there is now a certain amount of bad attitude involved on both sides.

Examples like this illustrate why dealing with your own organization is one of the secrets of excellent customer service. This customer service team could receive smile training on customer skills until they are blue in the face, and they would still harbor a great deal of resentment towards both these untrained customers and the sales department.

When you move past hypothetical examples to your own personal experiences as a customer, you might recall that many of your good and bad customer service experiences were organizational in nature. Consider the last time that you wanted something as a customer and the person that you dealt with would not provide it. Chances are it had less to do with their attitude and more to do with the constraints of their internal customer relationships. To serve you properly would have subjected them to criticism for taking too much time, using too many resources or bothering people who did not wish to be bothered.

Creating service-friendly internal customer relationships takes real work. Here are some of the factors involved.

Proper management oversight

Most fraternal bickering in an organization is actually the result of management failing to set the right priorities. If each of these groups was chartered by their management to help the other group as part of their job functions, they would be accountable for doing so. Instead, each of the groups above have management objectives which simply involve the production of sales or service, and both are frustrated when the other group is an impediment to these objectives.

Rewarding the right things

In the above example, the customer service group was rewarded only for good external service, not good internal service. Likewise, the sales department was rewarded for making a larger quota at the expense of a larger service burden. Such selling to untrained users may in fact be costing the company more in extra service than that revenue warrants. Stop and take a global view of each team's reward structure in order to create incentives for the right efforts.

Adequate resources

When there is a shortage of personnel, equipment or money -- or these resources are not managed properly -- conflicts can break out as groups fight to get resources for their individual needs.

My customer support center spent a large amount of its time on the phone. One day our company's financial department decided to switch to a discount long distance carrier without consulting us first. The result was many calls having to be re-dialed or connecting with poor quality. Eventually one team member summed up everyone's feelings by saying, "We don't have a phone problem: we have a window problem, because we're going to start throwing these phones out the window." Instead of having a battle between management's need to cut costs and my need to keep our staff from tearing their hair out, it made more sense for us to jointly seek better ways to cut costs without cutting quality. We soon dropped the discount carrier and focused on saving money elsewhere.

More common situations include large workloads coupled with inadequate manpower or equipment, resources shared between groups, and unforeseen demands. Much like group objectives, resource requirements need to be monitored and management with an eye towards the best interests of the entire organization.

A team orientation

Question the attitudes behind any organizational problem. When groups have a competitive or hostile stance towards one another, even good management and proper resources may not be sufficient to insure teamwork.

As a customer service manager, whenever we hired a new sales manager, anywhere in the world, they would get a visit or a phone call from me and a business card with both my work and home number on it. And I'd tell them, "If you ever need help with a product or demonstration, call me anytime, 24 hours a day. Your success is very important to us." Furthermore, I made it clear to my staff that I expected an equally positive attitude from them, beginning the moment they started working for me. By taking an active role in helping sales managers succeed, we could always count on their support as well.

The 105% rule discussed earlier in this book -- seek to exceed expectations by at least a little – applies well to internal customer relationships. When you dedicate yourself to keeping the rest of the company as happy as possible, the good you generate makes your job much easier than if you take a defensive posture towards others and work at cross purposes. As one Biblical passage says, a house divided against itself cannot stand. Likewise, an organization must recognize its essential internal relationships and work to nurture them.

Opening Up the Lines of Communication

Fostering good communication between groups is one of the best ways to build strong internal customer relationships. In the example above, the two warring parties would have resolved their differences more easily if they understood each other's concerns. The more openly information is shared among the various customers and suppliers within your working environment, the more cooperation there will be in setting objectives and meeting mutual goals. An open and frank atmosphere on all sides helps build the social relationships that form the underpinnings of a good working relationship. Two main lines of communication need to be cultivated within an organization:

Communications between management levels

This includes sharing information among management, and between management and employees. These channels can range from meetings and corporate newsletters to regular wandering around among the troops. It is particularly crucial for communication between management and people doing the work flow both ways, because each party has critical information the other party doesn't.

Communications between teams

These can range from formal channels such as inter-group meetings and company-sponsored activities to informal seminars, parties and friendly competition.

Both managers and employees have important information to share with one another in the course of their working relationship. Management has the operating responsibility for a group, and it sees the wider picture of where the group is heading and how it must fit in with company objectives. What makes a manager effective is the ability to take diverse people with specific talents and direct those talents towards the overall goal. In doing so, few things are more important than honest communication about the group's common goals and how each person is contributing to it.

Employees know how to do their job better than anyone else, and this expertise must be conveyed to management. Even the most powerful CEO of an industrial giant can't advise how to build a part better than the people who work with it every day on the production floor. Teams that respect the expertise and experience of everyone in the group and give everyone a chance to communicate, generate a great deal of respect and commitment from team members.

Building and maintaining good communication is a matter of providing the proper channels and using them. In practice, this can range from providing the resources for an internal employee newsletter, to scheduling regular meetings between teams, to making sure that senior managers keep their doors open on a regular basis. It's as much a matter of style as of procedure --

when it gets the proper attention, people feel more free to speak up and participate at all levels of the organization. In a customer service environment, it's particularly good to seek opportunities to educate others in the organization about customer issues, and help to build a more customer-friendly environment.

A prime objective in better corporate communications is to make sure that everyone understands the big picture of an organization's goals and how these goals relate to everyone's job. How many times, for example, have you had poor service because employees put petty rules and regulations ahead of the more important purpose of retaining you as a customer?

One recent article in Training Magazine (Nov. 1995) describes a case in which the authors asked a fast-food restaurant to serve them a sandwich without lettuce, and the employees refused to even remove the lettuce from an already-made sandwich. As the authors put it, "We reached a compromise – we removed the lettuce ourselves and left it on the counter, and they had to take the time to clean it up."[14]

Preventing "Over the Wall" Syndrome

Sometimes it seems that the flow of work is like a volleyball game, with problems being batted back and forth between people who don't want them to land on their desk. This over the wall syndrome has its roots in the reward structure between employees and their management. Anything that doesn't fall within the scope of how a person is judged or rewarded goes back over the wall for someone else to take care of.

A key way to get around the over the wall syndrome is to knock down as many walls as possible. Just as you need heavy equipment to knock down a real wall, you need tools to knock down corporate ones. The best tool of all is good management teamwork on the scope of every group's responsibilities and the work flow between groups. Beyond this, there are some other important tools.

Educate your organization

People who work with the public have much to teach the rest of the company, because they deal so closely with customers. You can teach others in the company how they can best avoid your most common customer problems. As customer relations experts, your team should be part of an integral feedback loop to the rest of the company, passing along what customers want, what they need, and how it affects the company's products, designs, and future plans.

Learn from the organization

On the other side of the coin, groups that work with the public must also learn as much as possible from the others in the organization. This shared resource of information works to make your job of dealing with customers more productive.

Seek positive ways to disagree

Sometimes groups will have to disagree, particularly when there is a conflict in resources or priorities. Handle these disagreements using the same diplomatic skills you develop with customers: communicate your interests, acknowledge the other party's interests, seek reasonable compromises, and never let the discussion get personal. Strive for positive, constructive ways of working with the other groups in your company that recognize both your needs and the greater good of the organization.

Scratch their back

If you work with customers, a good way to insure the long-term cooperation of other groups is to look out for the interests of these groups as well as your own. For example, offer to share manpower with other teams during their respective peak periods, or seek better ways to protect other people from customer interruptions as much as possible. If you make an effort to champion the interests of the rest of your organization, it will generally promote the kind of harmony that lets you get the job done quicker and better, and have more fun doing it.

> Such mutual relationships were one of the key factors in my own ability to keep a quality support operation running smoothly. For example, our firm had a training department that traveled constantly. In return for my group providing relief for some of their workload, their staff would cover the support hotline when we were short-handed due to vacations, illnesses or peak periods. But this relationship was much more than sharing resources; it enriched the careers of everyone concerned. Our people were able to get out from behind the phones and take company-paid trips all over the country, while the educational team kept current with our products, experienced customer feedback first hand, and got to spend more time home with their families.

Win-win situations benefit everybody and help your organization to approach its problems as a team.

Help your own people learn and grow in their jobs

Some organizations have a policy of having customer service people give cradle-to-grave care to a customer's problem, wherever possible. They get the answers to problems from the company's experts and discuss these answers with the customers themselves whenever possible.

With the right kinds of effort, one can take the natural differences between groups in an organization, and channel them into productive working relationships. A historical example of this is the story of American and British forces in the Pacific Northwest in the 1800's. After years of armed conflict, a truce was declared, and the two garrisons spent the remainder of their postwar years trying to outdo each other at lavish banquets. In perhaps the same way, gestures ranging from joint planning sessions to simple lunch invitations can knock down the walls standing between the objectives of different teams. While no organization ever experiences a complete absence of conflict, proactive management of your essential relationships can help keep these conflicts to a minimum and rechannel this energy toward positive outcomes.

Dealing With Difficult People at Work

You might feel that similar skills are needed in dealing with difficult customers and difficult co-workers. This is only partially true. For difficult customers, your goal is to bring a transaction to a close, with someone you may never see again. With people in your organization, you face the additional challenge of working with these people day in and day out.

There was once a rash of books and articles available describing "working with jerks," which certainly did strike a chord with many people in the workforce. It's best, however, to avoid portraying people as jerks. Personalities differ and often clash, but you can learn to manage these differences and strive for solutions where everyone wins. For that to happen, you have to start by not putting labels on people.

To find positive ways of resolving conflict within the workplace, the emphasis must be on building relationships, not just solving conflicts. To do this effectively, keep some of the following guidelines in mind.

Understand others
It is important to put yourself in the other person's shoes, look out for their concerns as well as yours, and develop the diplomacy to get past their attitudes to seek a solution.

Clear the air
Perhaps the worst thing that one can do with difficult peers is to let frustrations simmer under the surface, since too often they erupt later as open hostility. Be frank about disagreements in a matter that is constructive rather than confrontational. Above all, seek a mutual sense of understanding by listening intently to what the other party has to say and re-stating their concerns before continuing with your own.

Don't stereotype
There is no such thing as "bad people," only people who do things that you don't agree with. Concentrate on an individual's actions and not their personalities in getting things back on track.

Encourage positive changes
A curmudgeon is not likely to turn into a champion of positive thinking overnight. However, most of us are driven by praise and acknowledgement. When you notice and encourage small

changes in behavior, you sow good feelings and provide a base for that person to build upon.

Seldom will all people in an organization have the same personality and attitude as you do. A crowning touch in your organizational skills is the ability to work with other types of people and help them grow. Even among people with an "attitude," making them feel worthwhile is important, since often these problems stem from insecurity and a poor self-image.

One particularly sensitive internal customer relationship deserves special mention – your boss. It is important to be a partner, not a threat, to the person you report to. It makes logical sense not to put someone who decides about your raises and promotions on the defensive. Of course, this doesn't imply not being frank about your job and your feelings; it just means that here, particularly, it makes sense to keep the level of communication as positive and non- confrontational as possible.

At the same time, your relationship with every single person on the team is important to your career. The way you comport yourself with the most difficult people in your organization is a measure of your leadership abilities. Becoming known as a diplomat who can relate with everyone in your work environment goes a long way towards resolving day to day problems on the job, and helps you be more effective in taking a lead role where you work.

Today's Team Based Work Environments

As of this writing, a major change is sweeping many working environments throughout the world. Companies were once organized by function with, for example, a product design group, a manufacturing group, and a quality assurance group. Nowadays, firms are rapidly moving towards cross-functional teams, flexible environments based around projects rather than functions, where people can be deployed as needed. One early example was in the auto industry, where some major automobile manufacturers shifted from an assembly line to teams that took responsibility for assembling an entire vehicle.

This represents a major change in the social fabric of today's workforce. While work once went over the wall from one group to another, there is now a shared peer-group responsibility for an entire phase of a project. It also represents a major shift in management responsibility. There are now fewer bosses and more people empowered to make decisions on a team basis. While decentralizing authority can present a challenge to internal service and support, it also means that more individual employees are empowered with a greater amount of responsibility and authority than ever before.

For a customer service professional, the move towards a team-based workforce is both a challenge and an opportunity. On one hand, it may scatter your internal customer relationships among numerous individual projects. On the other hand, people in teams can have a greater sense of ownership in their group's product and thus provide better internal customer service. Here are some tips for getting the best support in this changing environment.

Build channels as well as relationships

Because teams often work under substantial pressures to meet their goals, and individual team members may view customer support as an interruption to their other tasks. It is particularly important to appoint people as liaisons for individual teams. Get management involved to formalize channels of customer service support from teams.

Respect individual agendas

In today's team-based environment, people are prone to being pulled in too many directions at once by conflicting demands, as opposed to the days of the hierarchical standard of one person, one boss. For problems that need more than a short consultation, get team leaders involved in any projects that require their resources.

Recognize everyone's importance

Now that individual team members are empowered to have expertise and authority in what they do, the concept of "management" is much more widely distributed than before. Today's team leader may be tomorrow's team member, and vice versa. This means that customer service professionals need to be sensitive in respecting the equal importance of team members when interacting or seeking assistance.

Today's team working environments have the potential for much better internal customer service over all. Team members often have a greater sense of the best interests of the whole organization, not just of their individual job functions. This new structure can also help create a multi-disciplinary base of expertise for the company and a more flexible allocation of resources where they are most needed. Managed well, working teams form a foundation where customer service professionals can function more effectively than ever.

The Case for Good Politics

When people think of organizational politics, it often has a negative connotation in peoples' minds. They think of back-room deals, old boy/girl networks, and battles for corporate turf. These simply represent undesirable extremes of a very important component to your working life – the social and interpersonal relationships on the job which help everyone work effectively to meet their goals.

> Several years ago, I had the privilege of taking sabbatical leave from my job as a customer service manager and spending a month in China as part of a World Bank educational project. One thing that stood out in working with the Chinese was their informal system of *guanxi* or network of favors given and received. Official business in China is often deeply entrenched in bureaucracy, but Chinese professionals, who are among the most resourceful and capable I've ever met, often have a "back door" of personal contacts needed to get things done. This *guanxi* is what greases the skids for much productive work accomplished in Chinese institutions.

Good advice for every customer service professional, whether on the front lines or in the executive suite, is to develop an enlightened sense of *guanxi* within your own organization. Actively seek to build relationships with the people you collaborate with, and champion their needs and agendas. Reach out to peers, management and front-line staff to build a social network that underlies everyone's official duties. These social relationships, combined with proper management oversight, are the keys to effective internal customer service.

Don't underestimate the importance of these internal customer relationships. When external customers do not get good service, they may go away unhappy from that particular transaction. When internal customers are poorly served, however, the results can be much more devastating. When corporate infighting leads one group to ignore the needs of another group, the end result might be less output, poorer quality products, and perhaps the kind of loss in market share which could lead to people losing their jobs. Even when the situation is less extreme, there is a cost in morale and lost productivity when internal customer relationships are not cared for on an equal footing with external ones.

Embrace a good sense of politics in what you do. This is an inclusive, non-discriminatory kind of "politics" where you seek to give people within your work environment the same kind of service that you provide your customers. When you make a conscious effort to develop good internal relationships, you will find that you are functioning in a much stronger and more positive working environment.

Managing Your Internal Customer Relationships

Good internal customer relationships are perhaps one of the most crucial elements in a service-driven company, but they are often the last thing many people associate with customer service. It is all too easy to look at good service as being isolated to front-line customer transactions, or worse, relegated to a "customer service" department.

This fact represents a strategic competitive advantage for you and your business. When you identify and manage strong internal customer relationships, it clarifies everyone's goals and priorities towards what is best for your external customers as well. It also brings the added benefit of a more positive, cooperative workplace, which in turn has a direct financial impact in areas such as productivity, morale and turnover.

These benefits are all yours for the cost of managing and cultivating these relationships, as an ongoing process that never ends. Doing this takes hard work, an open mind, and at sometimes no small amount of diplomacy. Particularly in today's business environment, where human and financial resources are often stretched to the limit, building a team approach to customer problems is not always the path of least resistance. However, when you and your organization get in the habit of doing it well, you will discover that it is the path to greatness.

Section III:

Personal Skills

Step 7:

Take Care of Your Most Important Customer

One of the most overlooked aspects of customer service is the relationship that you have with your most important customers: yourself. The concept of serving others by taking care of yourself is far from new. Many people have read the Biblical injunction to "Love your neighbor as yourself" to mean that you should treat others well. In reality, it has a dual meaning; in loving your neighbor "as" yourself, it states that you must love yourself as well. This advice has strong practical implications in today's world. You cannot give people excellent service when you are tired, burned out, dispirited or lack self-confidence. Conversely, the very best people professionals invariably have a lot of fun at what they are doing and feel great about themselves.

This chapter will look at some of the most important aspects of taking good care of yourself: managing your time, managing the level of stress that you feel in your work, and the broader issue of balancing work with the rest of your life.

Time pressures and job stress are epidemic in today's workforce. A recent survey showed that over 60 per cent of people feel high levels of stress at work, nearly 70 per cent of employees feel "spent" by the end of the work day, and a nearly equal percentage feel exhausted when they get up for work in the morning. This represents a tremendous waste of human energy and potential. There is no question that the pressures of today's working environment, with its high expectations and leaner staffs, contribute to this sad state of affairs. At the same time, it underscores the importance of developing your own personal tools for managing stress in your life and becoming assertive about using your talents on the job. When you learn to control the amount of stress you experience at work, you have developed an important tool for serving customers well and feeling good about yourself and your job.

Time Management

You have undoubtedly heard the axiom that time is one resource that, once spent, can never be recovered. More to the point for most people, it presents a finite limit to our daily efforts. A mismatch between the amount of work we feel that we must accomplish and the time available to perform it represents one of our greatest sources of stress.

Managing time effectively is often a two-step process: (1) make the most of the time you have, and (2) be assertively realistic, about what can be accomplished within a given amount of time. Customer service has its own unique time pressures: it often involves large quantities of transactions, a continuous need to balance immediate needs against longer-term action items, and people with a sense of urgency to solve their problems.

The good news is that everyone has a tremendous amount of hidden time stashed away in their day. Even the best of us can waste between two and four hours per work day, and we should all give ourselves some credit for being human. At the same time, there are techniques that most of us can use to painlessly add an extra hour or more to your day. First, let's take a look at one the most important time management tools: personal planning.

A Meeting with Yourself

Have you ever tried to read a map while you were driving? It is tough to pay attention to traffic and signs while struggling with how to reach your destination. Most of us take some time out to read the map first, then continue unhurried to the destination. The problem is, few of us apply the same logic to our working day.

This leads us to what may be the most important issue in time management for customer service professionals. Many of us come in each day and confront a desk full of undone work. We then flit from problem to problem, never getting much completely finished, and leave when the clock strikes five o'clock (or later). At the end of a week, a month, or a year, we really don't have a good explanation for why things didn't get done as quickly as we hoped. This often isn't a matter of being poor workers; rather, it's often just a matter of not stopping to read the map first. The average person's workday is the equivalent of trying to drive across a strange city with little forethought or planning.

Fortunately, one simple habit that can become as natural as brushing your teeth has the potential to unlock an almost unbelievable amount of productivity in your workday. What's more, it is a habit that is not only simple but pleasurable to follow. This key to working productively lies in scheduling regular time every day for a meeting with your most important customer: yourself.

Personally, I set aside five inviolate minutes at the beginning of the day to have a meeting with myself. During this meeting, I review where I stand in terms of both short and long term priorities, and what I can reasonably expect to get done today. The resulting list is my personal plan for the day, and its items are only things that occupy my attention unless a compelling reason for changing them comes along. Equally important is another five minute meeting with myself at the end of each business day to review what actually was done, what didn't get done (and why), and to add to the list any new items I spent time on that day. Finally, I save the lists. These slips of paper form an important planning document that tells me where I've been and where I'm going.

These slips, together with an ongoing list I maintain for future priorities, form the basis for weekly and monthly meetings with myself. At these meetings, the intention is to take a little more time and plan the long term priorities -- and review my rate of progress towards the goals I set previously.

The benefits of having a meeting with yourself are powerful: first of all, you channel your efforts towards known goals. When you look each morning at a full desk of paperwork, the natural tendency is often to flit aimlessly from problem to problem, never fully completing much. The meeting with yourself arms you with knowledge about the best use of your time. When you do it, you'll be positively amazed at how much more real work gets done. Second, you know exactly where you stand. In time, you develop a feel for your work habits, your usual rate of progress, and what you do best. This in turn gives you the ability to confidently predict what can be accomplished in the future. Finally, you have factual data to present to your management about your duties and goals. This raw data gives you a key edge in explaining why a project may be behind schedule, giving constructive advice on improving productivity, and, perhaps, even justifying a raise or promotion for yourself.

Many experts have emphasized the importance of having goals and writing them down. This latter point is particularly important, because putting a goal into writing represents a commitment, and this commitment almost always helps focus your efforts towards meeting that goal efficiently. This is why sources ranging from psychology textbooks to get-rich-quick tracts all emphasize the importance of written goals. Don't just think in terms of today's work; keep track of what you'd like to see over the next week, the next month, and the next year. These interim goals give you the feedback you need to keep your plans and progress on track.

So why doesn't everyone plan their time like this? Perhaps because of a misguided belief in the work ethic. The great irony of working life is that most people fail to plan -- and thereby plan to fail -- because somehow it doesn't feel right to be taking time off from getting your work done in the face of a large pile of demands. But in my experience, regular meetings with yourself, combined with the resulting to-do lists, has a tremendous impact on one's personal productivity on the job. Moreover, it gives you a great deal of visibility about how much you can get expect to get done in a day, and how to plan your time. Try it this week -- just for one week -- and see what a difference this simple technique makes in your own working environment.

A Few More Time Tricks

Beyond your own planning and tracking, there are a number of other techniques that can help you add time to your day and be smarter about your work. Discussed below are some other time management techniques that work well within a customer service environment.

Set priorities

In the computer science field, much research has been spent to help machines decide what resources to give among competing programs. These operating systems look at factors such as the number of demands there are on the computer's time and memory, who needs what resources, how long each program has been waiting, and then makes microsecond-by-microsecond decisions as to what should run when. Done well, everyone should end up running as efficiently as possible.

On a much broader scale, you can apply the same technique to the problems that are in your in-basket to service them more efficiently. Prioritize problems based on factors such as how long a customer has been waiting, who is on vacation and can wait, and how many problems can be resolved that particular day. On a broader scale, take a look at your longer-term priorities and plan how to attack these as well, for example, two hours per day every morning on your capital budget. When you invest a little advance time in setting priorities, it helps break down a large workload into day-size or even hour-size chunks, and helps you keep focused.

Optimize your use of work hours and time zones

Many things are more easily accomplished at certain times rather than others. At a personal level, this can mean solving your toughest problems during times of the day when you are at your intellectual peak, rather than struggling through them right after lunch, for example, when your metabolism is urging you to pitch face forward onto your desk. Moreover, there are times when people tend to be in meetings – Monday at 9 AM, in many environments, for example. Plan to contact people when they are most likely to be available or based on how much time you expect their transactions to take.

If you work with a national or global customer base, you can also arrange your contacts to optimize the use of regional time zones. If you are on the west coast of the United States, for example, you could call clients on the east coast (which is three hours later) in the early morning hours, then switch to the west coast when the east coast goes to lunch around 9 AM your time. Similarly, you can concentrate on the east coast again when the west coast goes to lunch – I personally took an earlier lunch hour for this purpose – finish up with east coast clients before they go home, and then concentrate on the west coast again for the rest of the day.

Take definitive action on paperwork

There is an honored time management principle in business which states that when you pick up a piece of paper on your desk, don't put it down again until you take action on it. At a practical level, this can make sense for short term paperwork items, but it is difficult if the piece of paper you just picked up details a four-week customer survey project. More pragmatically, it makes sense to get in the habit of practicing "triage" with your paperwork.

The term triage has its roots in emergency medical situations such as natural disasters, and in this context, it refers to the practice of dividing up victims into three categories: people who will die regardless of treatment, people who will live regardless of treatment, and people who will only live if they are treated now. The medics take care of the third group first, before tending to the other two. With the pile of paperwork on your desk, you can perform a similar triage. Put aside matters that you know won't be addressed today, discard paperwork that you never need to act on, and create a smaller set of action items that you can effectively act on today; then, focus your attention exclusively on that pile.

A related talent worth developing is the skill of proactively reducing the amount of paper in your life. Look at every memo and mailing that you get with an eye towards whether it can be discarded right now, so that you can reserve your valuable desk space for action items needing your attention. If you are a pack rat with a natural tendency to save everything, try putting a box next to your desk and dump everything into it that you might get to later. Then, once or twice a year, go through that box and toss out everything that you didn't really need -- which will usually turn out to be most of it.

Manage your customer's sense of urgency

While it is good professional practice to have guidelines for managing your daily workload, be sure to factor the human dimension into this equation. If someone needs something urgently, and that need is genuine, you should try to juggle your other priorities to meet these needs. A customer's sense of urgency, combined with the needs of the situation, are factors that deserve as much consideration as the problem itself. How well you do in the aggregate depends not only on how you take care of everybody, but also how well you take care of those people who feel their problem has a special urgency. This issue is one that can really separate the masters from the apprentices in dealing with the public.

In such cases, it's important to have techniques to say and do that will put your most time-pressured customers at ease. Make it clear what amount of attention the problem is getting from what level of people in your organization, and give it a sense of closure by summarizing the action items. Tell the customers exactly what you intend to do for them, when to expect a resolution to occur, and what they can do to check on the status of the problem.

From a time-management standpoint, it makes sense to plan ahead for all of the unpredictable interruptions that occur from urgent customer-driven situations, in much the same way that dentists leave room for a certain number of emergency visits each week. Use your past planning history to understand the impact of urgent interruptions on your workload, and schedule your daily activities to have enough leeway to deal with the ones which crop up in the future.

Multi-tasking

Multi-tasking is yet another computing term which refers to getting something done while waiting for something else to happen, for example, running one program while another one is waiting idly for the user to type something. A similar principle applies with human beings, in which you can manage your processor (your brain) to take advantage of all of the small breaks of down time that occur during the day when we get blocked on other tasks. For example, the time you normally spent on hold or waiting through a computer delay may be a good time to work on short, interruptible projects, such as reading correspondence or filling out logs. Planning certain jobs to be idle process tasks can help take many of them out of your regular schedule.

Given my own typically hectic workload, undertaking this book project involved some creative multitasking. For example, when I began writing it, I had a 45-minute commute on the freeways to work each way. As I started out for work, I would take an inexpensive voice-activated dictation recorder and flip it on as I started for work. Then I would just talk. Each day's commute would yield a good, solid hour of discussion on tape and would get the creative juices flowing for things to discuss during the next commute. Later, as the book was being completed, I would often bring a laptop computer along in the passenger seat as I rode along on road trips with my wife or business colleagues. Both ideas allowed me to pour a substantial amount of otherwise idle time into a project.

It helps a great deal if the tasks which fill up your so-called idle time are fun and relatively easy, so that you don't feel that you are taking on more drudgery in your spare time. Any good behavior can be taken to extremes, and it is important to make the distinction between working too hard and finding pockets of time that you can painlessly take advantage of, without breaking your stride, to get more done in your day. Looking for multi-task opportunities can add a substantial amount of productivity to your day.

Use your back burner

Sometimes the best way to deal with a problem is to forget about it, at least for a while. The phrase "to sleep on it" has more significance than many people realize. It is a truism in behavioral psychology that thinking about a problem before you go to sleep lets your subconscious mind work on an answer overnight. Personally, when I go to bed thinking about work problems, I often find that an answer comes to me in the shower the next morning.

In your daily work life as well, it is often possible to focus on a problem for so long that you lose perspective on how to solve it. Putting it aside and returning later with a fresh point of view can often be one of the most productive ways to solve a difficult problem. This is because disengaging our conscious attention from a problem often frees up our internal problem-solving skills and memory. How many times, for example, have you struggled to remember someone's name, then given up, only to have the name suddenly appear out of the blue several minutes later? Regular breaks and diversions can become an important part of solving difficult problems on the job.

It is important here not to confuse a creative pause with long, arbitrary project delays, particularly when customers are waiting. At the same time, managing a particular day or week's tasks to take breaks and move from one task to another can lead to more efficient use of your time, compared with continually slogging away even when you are stuck.

Assertively Manage Your Workload

Most of the advice given above treats the size of your workload as a given, but it is perhaps even more important to develop the negotiating skills to keep this workload in line with your ability to service it properly. Sadly, the overextended employee has become a fact of life in many working environments, particularly in today's economic times. Downsizing and consolidation often leave fewer people servicing more work. Even in the best of organizations, it is easy for top performers to keep having tasks added to their agenda.

This means that you need to take steps to manage your own workload levels, both for your own good and for the good of your organization. Doing this well requires a certain level of diplomacy and assertiveness. With today's cost-pressured environment, it means keeping track of your own personal productivity and being able to come up with creative solutions which maximize this productivity within the bounds of a reasonable workday. One positive approach to take with your management, for example, is to present suggestions for reducing less critical work items, or distribute critical tasks among various parts of the organization.

Sometimes, all that you need to do is speak out; often, managers won't know that someone is overextended until they say so. This can be particularly difficult for customer service professionals, who are by nature eager to please those around them as work keeps piling up, but it is better to learn to speak out than to disappoint everyone in the long run through burnout or poor productivity. In other situations, you may need to make a case for improvements, such as better resources or more realistic schedules, and justify these against the realities of your workload. Either way, good management of the demands made upon you inevitably becomes an important part of your overall effectiveness. Above all, make sure that you take action to protect your own time and productivity at work.

Take your vacation
Avoid falling into the trap of working to the point of cashing in your vacation as extra pay. There are many ways to make

money, but you never can make even a single additional moment of time. Use the precious gift of time for yourself and your loved ones, and you'll often be surprised to find an extra added bonus of better productivity at work.

Come in early and leave on time

Coming in early lets you do your best work uninterrupted in the early part of the day, when most people are at their freshest. Also, it sends a signal to your management and the rest of the company that you are eager to get to work, while staying late can send a signal that you aren't keeping caught up with your work.

Don't work gratuitous overtime

There are times in almost any job where people need to rise above and beyond the call of duty to meet an important deadline -- that's teamwork. But people constantly working late isn't always good for the organization, both in terms of morale and in terms of one's aggregate efficiency overall. As a manager, I have seen things work best when people practice good time management and give their very best during regular working hours, and then go home.

If you are a manager, put the shoe on the other foot as well, and resist the temptation to squeeze every bit of overtime possible out of your troops. Beyond the ethical issue of fair employee treatment, and the fact that people are entitled to lives outside of their working hours, this is in your economic self-interest. Compare excessive workloads with the cost of turnover and constant retraining, and the much greater intangible costs of putting frustrated, overworked people in front of your customer base, and you should understand that it makes good business sense to keep every person's workload in line with reality.

Stress Management for Service Professionals

Stress is a fact of life, and at times particularly so in the workplace. However, most people have more control over stress than they think. The most surprising fact to realize about stress is that it is not -- repeat, not -- caused by external events in your life. Every waking emotion that we have is a result of our internal interpretation of what happens around us, and what thoughts we have based on these perceptions.

Well-known psychologist Dr. Albert Ellis has made a career of pointing out the cognitive mistakes that often guide our thoughts. He describes three steps he calls the ABC's that outline the process many of us go through in creating stress for ourselves.[15]

- An *Activating event* happens. For example, a customer is rude to us.
- Next, we filter this activating event through an irrational *Belief* system. "He probably thinks I'm doing a lousy job. Next, he might complain to my boss. Then I'll be fired. And then I'll never get a job again. And I'll be eating out of dumpsters for the rest of my life. And ...."
- Finally, we suffer the *Consequences* of these irrational beliefs, in the form of stress, worry and dysfunctional behavior.

According to Ellis, it is the irrational belief that causes stress, not the activating event. There are two problems with these beliefs. First, they may not be correct; the customer might have been curt because of a fight with his spouse, or indigestion, or perhaps a snub from another colleague. Second, even when there is some truth to our observations, we take them to lengths that are inappropriate and unhelpful.

Suppose that the customer was in fact upset by something that we did or said. It is still probably incorrect to presume that we will be fired. Even if we were going to be fired, it is neither correct nor helpful to presume that we are unemployable. In all likelihood, neither is the case in reality. Good management of these stresses involves proactively challenging these negative thoughts and changing them to more rational ones.

With the above situation, you might instead remind yourself that the customer could be in a bad mood for reasons having nothing to do with you. Or if there is a problem between the two of you, seek positive ways to communicate and resolve these problems.

These cognitive principles of behavior have become the cornerstone of much of the modern counseling strategy for problems such as depression. In a customer service environment, they serve as an important tool to detach yourself, and your professional skills, from the emotions that can surround you in a customer transaction. Here are some ways to put these into practice:

- As you deal with customers, envision yourself as a sociologist, observing the "tribal behavior" of customers with the detached interest of a researcher.
- Learn to respond to emotionally-charged statements by re-stating the customer's feelings, and then responding with neutral, professional statements of your own. This does not mean being cold and distant nor withholding empathy for the customer's situation. However, it also does not mean rising to the bait which may be thrown your way.
- Keep your focus on solving the customer's problem, from a standpoint of both their self-interest (obtaining a solution) and yours (closing the transaction).

The key point here is that developing the habit of responding professionally instead of emotionally is an effective way to stress-proof yourself from the vast majority of customer transactions. Compare the following two approaches.

Customer: You idiots said that this would be fixed! What's the matter with you people? Can't you get this right?
Service: Look, people are busy and overworked here, and most people don't complain as much as you do. What do you want us to do?

Few service professionals would have initially set out to say what was just said here. What happened is that the service person got flustered and angry, and made the mistake of responding at a personal level. The result of shooting from the hip like this rarely gets you or your organization out of the transaction successfully. Here is a more cognitive approach.

Customer: You idiots said that this would be fixed! What's the matter with you people? Can't you get this right?

Service: You sound very unhappy with the quality of our repair. If you would like, I can see to it that our chief technician personally makes sure this is fixed right this time. Would you be willing to leave this with us again?

Customer: I wanted it fixed right this last time.

Service: I can understand that. What would you like us to do to make it right?

Customer: Well, can you make sure that I get this back tomorrow.

Service: Certainly. I apologize that you had to bring this back again, and I'll make sure that this is ready for you tomorrow.

The payoff here is that when you learn to handle transactions like these cognitively, instead of emotionally, you will often find that your angriest customers will come away thinking very highly of you. When people lose their cool in a public situation -- as most of us have done ourselves, from time to time -- they don't expect to receive a kind and professional response. When they do, it often makes a very strong positive impression. Learning this kind of response strategy will make all of your transactions, angry or not, go much more smoothly and reduce the amount of stress you experience on the job.

How to Manage Your Own Stress Level

Did you know that it impossible to be anxious when your muscles are physically relaxed? There is a strong mind-body connection between your state of mind and the amount of muscular tension that you carry around physically. Learning to notice stress in your own body and how to deal with it can be an important tool in your own stress management arsenal.

Most modern tranquilizing drugs, including alcohol, primarily function as muscle relaxants. Many psychotherapeutic treatments for anxiety disorders involve learning and practicing deep states of relaxation. These same techniques can be used on the job and in your personal life as an effective, chemical-free way of releasing stress levels within your body and mind.

There are resources available in most communities for learning ways to manage your own stress, in the form of classes, counseling or even on-the-job programs. Beyond these, there are many ways to take action on your own to reduce tension and feel better on the job. When you start to feel some of the physical sensations of stress -- such as a tight throat, nervous stomach, excessive sweating, blurry vision, or feelings of anxiety -- try using some of the techniques below to reduce your stress to a more tolerable level.

Deep breathing

Deep breathing skills are a cornerstone of stress management, for a good physical reason. When we are under stress, people tend to take short, shallow breaths from high up in our chest, as if we were preparing to run away. This upsets the balance of carbon dioxide and oxygen in our bloodstream, and contributes to physical sensations of being nervous and out of control.

Learning to breathe slowly and naturally is one of the easiest ways to control many of the feelings that come with stress as well as help us to feel a sense of ownership over our own bodily reactions. Practice the following exercise as a quick way to calm down in a stressful situation. Close your eyes and inhale slowly and deeply, to the count of five. Keep your chest still as you breathe in, inhaling from your diaphragm at the base of your rib cage. Hold this breath for a count of three, then exhale slowly from your diaphragm to the count of five. Repeat three times.

Quick muscle relaxation

Take a slow, deep breath, and then tighten the muscles of the lower part of your body. Feel the tension from your feet up through your thighs and hips, and try to get in touch with as many muscle groups as possible. Hold this tension for a count of five, and then release it as you exhale slowly and deeply.

Repeat this process, but tighten and release your other major muscle groups in the same inhale-tighten-hold-release-exhale cycle: first, your abdominal muscles, then your back (a key to bodily relaxation), your upper trunk (chest, shoulders, neck, arms and hands), and finally your facial muscles and scalp.

Full-body deep relaxation

When you are especially frazzled, inducing a deep state of relaxation can provide both temporary relief and an opportunity to regain your perspective. This kind of exercise is best done at home, either lying on the floor or comfortably seated in a reclining chair.

First, make yourself as physically comfortable and unrestrained as possible. Take off items such as your belt or eyeglasses, and loosen tight clothing. Next, close your eyes and take five deep breaths from the diaphragm: inhaling to the count of five, holding for three beats, then slowly exhaling to the count of five.

Starting with your toes, progressively work your way up your body and tighten, then relax that muscle group. Tighten while inhaling slowly and deeply, hold to the count of three, and relax while slowly exhaling. As you proceed, concentrate on each of the following muscle groups, your toes (curling inward), ankles and calves, thigh muscles, pelvis and buttocks, abdomen, back, chest, shoulders, upper arms, forearms, hands, neck muscles, mouth, nose, eyes, and scalp.

Now, explore this state of relaxation within your mind. With your eyes still closed, count slowly and silently from one to five, each time sinking into a deeper level of relaxation. Finally, count slowly back from five to one, each time getting closer to full consciousness. At the count of one, open your eyes. You will feel deeply relaxed and refreshed.

Exercise

Exercise has many direct benefits in stress control. A good workout, a run or even a brisk walk can help leave you relaxed afterwards, and a regular program of exercise can help to improve your general physical well-being, which, in turn, increases your resistance to stress. Exercising releases endorphins, natural brain chemicals that help create a sense of well-being. For people who get into the habit of exercising regularly, these good feelings generate enough enjoyment that they often hate to miss their regular workout. Corporations often encourage these habits by providing accommodations such as shower rooms and flexible lunch breaks.

A couple of cautions are in order with any exercise program: consult a physician first, particularly if you are over 35 or out of shape, and don't overdo things, especially in the beginning. It's always a good idea to get professional advice from trainers or other exercise partners, for a sense of how to pace yourself and what level of effort to work up to. Above all, choose an activity that you find pleasurable, so that you will stick with it.

Talk it out

Anxiety generally has two components: physical reactions to a perceived threat, and emotional reactions to messages you send yourself about a situation. You can start managing the physical side of this equation with techniques such as the deep breathing, muscle relaxation and exercise mentioned above. To deal with the emotional side of stress, however, it is equally important to get to the root of what is bothering you.

It is good to have trusted friends and colleagues with whom you can talk frankly about what's on your mind. Bringing problems out in the open can put them in a light where you can understand them better and start taking positive action to solve them.

For example, if encounters with too many angry customers are driving you nuts, a good, frank discussion could help you to seek better skills training for yourself, or perhaps improvements in company procedure that help cause fewer people to be angry in the first place.

More importantly, talking out your concerns gives other people a chance to add their perspective as well. If you feel overwhelmed by your workload, and you find that other people feel as swamped as you do, you will realize that you are far from alone or unusual and perhaps take action with your management to forestall a group burnout.

Reward Yourself

Of course, there is more to life than the work that you do. You need to actively make time for yourself and your interests. Time spent recharging your batteries is an important investment in your customer service skills, and not just during an annual vacation, but every day of the week.

In my early years as a customer service manager, I faced a heavy load of interpersonal transactions each and every day. While the work was tremendously enjoyable, it required a high level of intensity, non-stop, for days and at times stretched into the evening. I took an active approach to blocking out time for myself. At least once or twice a day, I would find an empty room (usually the basement computer room) and sit in silence to review the day and gain my bearings. In addition, lunch hour took on near-religious significance for me. One of the benefits of working in suburban Los Angeles was the proximity to a host of fine dining spots, and daily lunch alone at a nice restaurant was sacrosanct for me. Moreover, I made it a point to reserve one day a week for a truly fine meal in a setting such as luxury hotel.

This lunchtime ritual accomplished two important things. First, it served as a daily reminder to myself that I was doing a great job and deserved to treat myself well. Second, it was a refreshing break from the intensity of the job. After spending an hour eating a gourmet meal, then sitting under a hotel fountain reading the *Los Angeles Times*, I was more than ready to jump back into the lion pit again for another highly-charged afternoon of work.

Your circumstances may be different. You may work far from a great restaurant, prefer to be with friends, or punch a half-hour time clock for lunch. Nevertheless, the principle remains the same: you must take time, each and every day, to do something to be good to yourself. Whether this takes the form of a walk or jog, a lunchtime game of cards with your co-workers, or even the case of one co-worker who would regularly tote a cello into a conference room to relax, it is important to seek regular moments of pleasure in each and every work day. There are also other important strategies for keeping yourself fresh.

- Build up a healthy camaraderie and support system among peers. Start a mutual admiration society for each other's work and goals. Good human relations with your peers are among the key factors in how much you enjoy coming to work. Conversely, poor human relations can be one of the principal causes of burnout on the job.
- Reward yourself with your favorite reinforcers, whether favorite snacks at the desk, extra-special restaurants on lunch breaks, or periods of time for quiet reflection and planning.

These habits stoke your natural coping mechanisms and help you get into the habit of being kind to yourself at work.

- Nothing succeeds like success. Set goals for yourself -- keep them small at first, particularly if you feel mired in work -- and be sure to pat yourself on the back or give yourself some kind of tangible reward as you reach these goals.

In a very real sense, taking positive action to build regular doses of rewards and encouragement into your work is one of the most effective means of keeping stress under control. It recognizes the fact that you are important, and that your contributions on the job are worthy of your own respect and appreciation.

When You Need More Than a Quick Fix

Methods like the ones discussed above belong in every service professional's tool kit and when put into practice can have a noticeable effect on the overall level of stress one feels on the job. At the same time, there are situations that demand more than simple first aid. In particular, ongoing situations that cause internal conflict can have an impact on how you feel each day and how effective you are at work.

These situations can involve problems both on and off the job, and can range from a deep personality conflict with a supervisor to an ill relative or troubled child at home. Moreover, clinical problems such as alcoholism, depression, chronic anxiety or phobias affect a certain percentage of all people, regardless of their profession or working situation. Handled with the right kinds of attention and a supportive atmosphere from one's management, many of even the more serious problems can be dealt with to minimize their impact on one's working life.

When things become overwhelming, the first step should be a frank discussion with one's supervisor or human resources department. If the problems are job-related, keep the tone as positive as the situation allows, and propose solutions where possible; for example, instead of telling your boss that "I hate your slave driver attitude," talk about how you want to be as productive as possible and how you feel you could work better with less criticism.

For more personal problems, the first stop might be an outside counselor or clergy member, and many firms also offer employee assistance programs (EAP) offering advice on a confidential basis. While you need not share intimate details of personal problems with people in your organization, it is important to let your management know when problems are interfering with your work and seek out available solutions such as counseling or treatment.

Similarly, as a manager, it is important to know when an employee's behavior on the job might point to emotional or work-related problems, and give that person a chance to talk about it. It is crucial in these cases to present a non-threatening, helpful atmosphere, and to do a lot more listening than talking. Be aware that not all employees will open up under these circumstances and that your employees have a right to privacy about their personal lives. At the same time, you should make clear what work-related problems you have observed, and be positive and empathetic in offering help.

If the situation is job related, these problems are often best dealt with in the open between the affected parties, perhaps with you acting as an intermediary when there is open confrontation involved. For more personal problems such as health or family related concerns, you might refer an employee to resources such as an employee assistance program, health providers, or local counseling programs. In cases like these, be sure to enlist the cooperation of your organization's human resources department. In any case, your positive support can be an important factor in returning a troubled employee to full productivity.

Managing Your Customer Service Career

For most people, their jobs represent a place where they spend at least half of their waking hours. This means that there is an important payoff in developing long-term career goals, and turning your customer service job into a profession. The skills that you develop in creating good service experiences can serve you well at any level of the career ladder that you desire.

We live at a time in history where the service sector of the economy has become a primary source of jobs, versus traditional areas such as manufacturing. Moreover, customer service has become a growing competitive factor for firms in every type of industry. These trends mean that there is unparalleled opportunity for people who choose to work in the customer service profession. It also means that good career planning is an important part of reaching the personal goals that you set for your working life.

There are three key aspects to managing your own career in the customer services field:

- Evaluate your own interests in the field.
- Set goals and priorities for both your current position and long-term plans.
- Know how to apply your own customer service skills in the career development process.

This last point is important. In a very real sense, the people you serve in your work represent internal customers. Your daily working life can be seen as a larger scale series of transactions where their needs and your services are negotiated and delivered. For example, in your early career, you may provide your employer "customer" with quality servicing of 40 customer transactions per day; later, when you are developing as a manager, you may be leading a team of people to control costs and deliver measurable service quality goals.

Whatever level of work that you aspire to, when you combine your own career goals with good management of the relationships and services needed to meet these goals, your prospects of success are extremely good.

Is Customer Service Work For You?

Many, if not most, people reading this book will have some level of involvement with the customer service field. Nonetheless, many people can perform a job adequately without being in love with it, while others in the same position blossom in time to discover that they have nurtured a previously untapped potential. A first step in your own personal career planning is the look at the realities of the customer service field to see how it fits with your long-term professional goals.

Some traits tend to be common to successful customer professionals, therefore questions such as the ones below can serve as a good litmus test for checking one's basic temperament against the field as a whole. The more yes affirmative answers you can honestly give, the more likely you are to be comfortable with customer service as a long-term profession.

Test your "personality fit" for customer service work

I tend to be energized by interpersonal transactions.
>YES ___ NO ___

I communicate well with others.
>YES ___ NO ___

Customer problems do not bother me personally.
>YES ___ NO ___

I basically like most people.
>YES ___ NO ___

I can balance multiple priorities and see each to completion.
>YES ___ NO ___

In a crisis, I can keep a clear head.
>YES ___ NO ___

I can break bad news with tact and diplomacy.
>YES ___ NO ___

I can deal with unreasonable requests pleasantly and assertively.
>YES ___ NO ___

I often can find a creative solution to a problem.
>YES ___ NO ___

I get along well with my co-workers.
>YES ___ NO ___

At the same time, no group of questions can replace "the gut test": how you feel about your profession on a daily basis. No field is perfect, and even the best jobs will have their share of bad days. At the same time, it's good to step back from time to time and reflect on how much pleasure, or lack thereof, your work with customers is giving you.

Suppose that your response to this kind of reflection is, "Overall, the customers are great. I just dislike the people I'm working with." This is good because you have clarified where to devote your energies from here, either in taking steps to forge good communication and a better working relationship with them, or in seeking a better working environment which values your customer skills. Similarly, having the insight that you are basically happy with most aspects of your job can help you plan to build on your current position as a base for future responsibilities. Either way, this kind of self-knowledge is an important step before undertaking decisions about something as important as your career.

Taking a Proactive Approach to Career Planning

Career planning is generally a multi-stage process for most successful people: giving the best performance possible in your current position, setting longer term career goals, and taking steps which move you closer to these goals over time. A key aspect to this is viewing your current position as not just being a job but part of your career. Here, your current position and past experience can be seen as points along a path, and good career management involves taking a broad view of where this path is leading.

Much of the literature about career planning concerns the mechanics of the process such as setting goals, keeping track of when to expect promotions, when to change jobs, and so forth. This is important knowledge to have. At the same time, above this is a basic, guiding principle in that employees who give extra at their current jobs are the most likely to be promoted, be sought after by other companies, or even successfully switch careers. In short, the 105 percent rule that we discussed earlier in this book applies here as well.

New employees in particular, because of relative inexperience in the working environment, can easily fall in the trap of appearing more concerned about their long-term career than they are about pulling their weight in their present position. It can be easy in one's early career to view a company as an entity that should take care of you. With time, particularly in today's competitive environment, it becomes easier to understand the importance of putting our own daily contributions first. If you find you are only giving 85 percent on the job, you have to look in the mirror and ask yourself if you are in the wrong kind of work environment or if there are things you can do to make the current one better.

There are times when it's the first issue. It is hard to excel in an unsupportive environment where there isn't adequate reward for what you are doing. If you have tried your best to be a positive, creative influence and still did not succeed, you may be justified in patting yourself on the back for your efforts then gracefully moving on. But make sure to take a hard look at the second issue. It is easy to perceive a boss or co-worker as uncooperative while missing the fact that we've complained and put them on the defensive, rather than offering positive win-win resolutions to problems. It's also easy to misread the intentions of superiors -- what may seem picky to one person may be success-oriented perfectionism to another. One of the best litmus tests for gauging the potential of your working environment is to give an all-out commitment to hard work and a positive attitude and then evaluate the results.

Another factor in career planning is your own goals. Everyone has different things that really motivate them. For some it is responsibility, while for others it's money, and still others want to make a contribution to their industry or society. Goals are relative, and it is perfectly OK to simply want a secure paycheck and time with your loved ones. The importance of a goal is in how well it aligns with the things that you really love to do.

Above all, it is important to remain aware of these goals in your daily life. The late Maxwell Maltz's classic book *Psycho-Cybernetics* points out that if you have a goal, and keep that goal conscious within your mind, your subconscious mind will go to work in ways to move you towards that goal[16]. Let's say, for example, that you want to someday become the CEO of a company like yours. (Not a bad goal – a surprising number of today's corporate leaders come from the ranks of customer service.) You probably will not wake up tomorrow and become the CEO But if this goal guides your career plans, it may lead to steps in the appropriate direction such as:

- Learning about the concerns of your company's senior management.
- Finding a mentor within your company.
- Taking night school courses to earn an MBA.
- Seizing opportunities to demonstrate leadership.
- Understanding the profit and loss implications of your group's functions.

More importantly, having a goal will help guide the many smaller decisions that you make each and every day. For example, the next time you are tempted to criticize something that your boss did, you may instead research and propose a better solution that makes you both look good.

Jan Carlzon, the former head of Scandinavian Airlines Systems, once described each business day as consisting of tens of thousands of "moments of truth," where individual decisions and customer experiences shaped the overall perception and success of his company[17]. Having clear goals is an important means of guiding these moments of truth in your own career.

Career planning is partly something you do but also something that is a by-product of giving your best at your current job -- even if you plan to leave it someday. When you not only work hard, but rise above your own responsibilities to help solve the larger problems in your working environment, your industry often wants you to advance; good people with leadership skills are still sought after in most environments. In this sense, doing a quality, pro-active job in your daily position can help put much of the career planning process on autopilot.

Keeping Your Life in Balance

Your life is like a three-legged stool, with the three legs being your career, your social life, and your spiritual life. If any of these three legs gets disproportionate to the others, your life gets out of balance. Amidst the demands of today's workforce, you need to be proactive in making time for the life beyond your job and career.

Personalities and situations differ, so you need to match the attention you bring to your relationships off the job with the needs of the individuals in those relationships. Some people even thrive with a large amount of personal independence. I knew one colleague who traveled constantly, while his wife and children spent their summers at a beach home in another state. For them, they felt that this arrangement worked well, with periodic weeks and weekends together providing adequate emotional sustenance. Cases like these are probably exceptions to the norm. In most relationships, people need to spend regular amounts of time nurturing each other and sharing their lives outside of work.

Lack of attention to the family is a major problem among people who work, especially among talented people who care about their careers. The important thing here isn't measured in absolutes -- there will always be people who throw themselves into their career, and those for whom work is simply a means to an end to spend time with their families. In either case, the central issue is frank and open communication with people in the family regarding their needs for attention and nurturing, and a sincere effort on all sides to meet those needs.

Too often one's children get short shrift from their parents because of the pressures of making a living. Again, there are personal differences here, and your teenage children may want to be left alone as fervently as your five year old wants you to read him a story. The best response in both cases is to have an open mind and an open ear to your children.

Finally, in today's do-it-all era, you must make sure to carve out a certain amount of time that is yours and yours alone. Those things which place demands upon your time -- be it your work, your family, your civic activities, or whatever else -- can all easily grow to use whatever amounts of time that they can have from your life. Learn to set appropriate limits. Never forget that you are the sole manager of your own time and life.

Keeping It All in Perspective

Today's working environment demands a great deal from people, particularly in the customer service profession. Knowing how to manage your time and stress levels on the job are an important part of functioning at your peak and feeling confident in your abilities on the job. This chapter represents just a small tip of the iceberg on techniques to help you function better.

Other resources include books, tapes and related products available through the business or psychology sections of your bookstore, as well as training programs or counseling sessions available through work or in your community.

Perhaps the most important point to make on this subject is that when you learn to practice good time, stress and goals management on your job, you also learn to practice it in your life. The same skills that help you survive and flourish in your working environment can work just as well off-hours, in the way you deal with your family, your friends, and the general public at large.

Like many things in life, techniques such as the ones presented here become more useful with practice, and with time can become assimilated into your daily habits. It is never too late to learn new skills to help manage your professional life, and even small investments in your own personal development can pay large dividends in the long run.

Summary:

Delivering Legendary Customer Service in Your Business

Legendary customer service is both an art and a science. If there is a common denominator between companies that truly deliver legendary customer service, and a unifying theme across the seven steps in this book, it is that world-class customer service involves much more than simply being nice to people. It is an overall culture that affects the work of every person in an organization, and not just those who interact with customers on the front lines. It often begins as a strategy to succeed in the marketplace, and eventually becomes a way of life that motivates people to succeed in their own lives and careers.

In closing, we will look at some of the trends that are shaping the cultures of legendary service organizations today, and share some thoughts on using these seven steps in harmony to provide a workplace that consistently benefits your customers, your employees and your bottom line.

Trends driving today's legendary service cultures

While customer service itself is a timeless virtue, the tools needed to deliver it every day never stand still. Between competition, market pressures and a growing base of insight into organizational behavior, many new trends have emerged in the quest to create a consistent, excellent customer experience. As a result of these trends, customer service and support has become a very exciting field to be in right now, and one of the hottest growth professions in industry. As of this writing, four key areas stand out as being critical to the growth of quality service in today's market:

- Service process improvement
- Cross-functional training
- The growth of teams
- Customer support automation

Let's take a look at each of these areas in detail.

Service process improvement
Successful firms today are taking a fresh look at their service operations, and seeking ways to decrease costs and improve efficiency. In some cases, they are making radical alterations in

the way that they do business. In other cases, they may design their operations from the ground up around a service concept. Most service improvement projects are not simply a matter of finding ways to do existing tasks better; they represent an entirely new look, based on the customer's needs, on what business processes should be in the future.

The case of Southwest Airlines is an interesting one. Their on-line site features a short message from their chairman Herb Kelleher, and what do you think it covers. How service-focused they are? The importance of air transport? No. It primarily discusses the importance of "turning around" an aircraft quickly between arrival and departure, something which they do almost twice as fast as most of their competitors. Southwest competes successfully with higher-cost, higher fare airlines by working more efficiently while providing a great customer experience.

Southwest is famous for both its low fares and its excellent service. "War stories" include cases such as the time a ticket agent offered to fly along with an unaccompanied elderly passenger, or when a flight attendant put up a stranded passenger at her house. Its hiring procedures and reward structures help develop a highly motivated workforce with legitimate career paths. But above all, Southwest's reputation revolves around a system of efficient aircraft utilization, ticketing procedures and team working relationships that allow it to perform the near-miraculous task of providing high service quality at a low cost. This system, refined over years of experience, represents the key to its spectacular profitability in a competitive market.

Cross-functional training

Ever since the dawn of the Industrial Revolution, workers have often become specialized to the point where they spend their entire careers performing one narrowly defined job function. This is changing. Today, service professionals are increasingly becoming flexible resources to be deployed where needed, while developing a broad range of skills in the process. For example, service team members may have rotational duties in areas such as training, staffing service hotlines, product testing or marketing support, depending upon the needs of the company. Particularly in environments with seasonal or peak needs, flexible skills can become an important competitive tool.

Developing cross-functional skills is also an important strategy for enhancing the individual careers of people. It must be employed judiciously, and with concern for the particular talents and preferences of each employee. Having everyone try do everything is a common mistake, and one which can lead to turnover when people are forced outside of their comfort zone of capabilities. At the same time, many people will view learning the right kinds of skills as an opportunity for personal development.

Implemented properly, cross-training has the potential to be a win-win situation for everyone on the organization. It does require an investment in training – as much as 20% of a first-year team member's time – and close cooperation between affected managers. But a flexible pool of multi-talented people can allow companies to react quickly to changes in workload and market conditions and to save money by reducing duplication of resources. It can also help people become experts who understand many aspects of your organization, which in turn benefits your customers. More importantly, these skills can lead to the kind of career growth that helps your top performers make a long-term commitment to your organization.

The growth of teams

Once upon a time, we had a world of bosses and subordinates. Today, the lines of managerial authority are more complex. It is not unusual now to find leadership delegated to a working group, with team members who may be project leaders for one effort and team members for another. As with cross-functional training -- which often plays an integral part in a team environment -- the use of teams allow both expertise and project authority to be delegated in a flexible manner as needs change. Perhaps the best-known examples of teams are in the automotive manufacturing industry, where groups of workers take responsibility for an entire vehicle and have the authority to stop the production line when they spot a problem.

In a service environment, teams have the advantage of distributing authority where it is needed to serve customers. For example, the front-line customer service agents at an airline may have the authority to spend up to a certain amount of money to resolve a passenger's problem, based on their judgment of the situation. Having greater authority not only empowers them to do what they feel is best but also frees up service managers from having to approve routine transactions. In other industries, service teams may be chartered to take complete cradle-to-grave responsibility for a customer request, or have the authority to put a multidisciplinary group of people to work on solving a problem.

Getting teams to work requires a high level of commitment and buy-in from the members involved. Since performance and its rewards are often judged for the group as a whole, there tends to be a higher level of self-motivation from team members for everyone to perform well. There are pitfalls as well. The diffuse responsibility structure of teams requires careful management oversight. With fewer pre-ordained managers, there are pressures to maintain realistic career paths for talented employees. Nonetheless, the trend towards more distributed authority and decision making has the potential to benefit both customers and the bottom line.

Customer support automation

Automation is helping many customer support operations move from being the complaint department to becoming the nerve center of corporate information. Louise Kirkbride, a support automation pioneer, describes this era of automation as one where shared customer service data makes "every person the right person" when a customer has a problem. The resulting knowledge base becomes mission-critical information for the company as a whole. Supporting this trend is a young, high growth industry whose main component areas include:

- Logging and tracking customer transactions,
- Problem follow-up so that no one falls through the cracks,
- Knowledge bases of information supplied by past contacts,
- Integrating customer service data with other parts of the organization, and
- Sophisticated telecommunications tools to better route and manage customer requests.

More recently, tools such as the Internet and fax response systems have allowed many customers to help themselves to services. As one recent example, computer networking vendor Cisco Systems makes extensive use of the World Wide Web as a means for customers to find solutions to problems, check orders, and download software products directly. As a result of this investment, Cisco estimates that 70 per cent of their customer support and over $200 million per year of software sales are now transacted on-line.[18]

Technologies such as these continue to drop in cost to the point where even the smallest organizations can afford tools such as a call tracking system on their personal computers or a question-and-answer page on the World Wide Web. These technologies have the same potential for misuse as any other tool -- such as the case where a human being is replaced by an endless litany of phone menus. Yet on the whole, they represent a revolution in providing responsive service to customers.

A common thread throughout all these trends is that keeping customers satisfied requires a system that can back up the best efforts of its team members. Put another way, businesses can gain or lose massive amounts of customers based on whether they have a competitive infrastructure for providing quality service.

In the early 1980s, a few firms all but dominated the then-fledgling market for personal computer software. Back then, many of these companies felt that they were in the software business, not the service business. If you needed support, you had to go to your dealer from assistance. This decision cost less in the short run, because these vendors didn't need to maintain expensive technical support departments for their end users. At the same time, it left customers at the mercy of their individual dealer's customer support skills that, in those early days, weren't always very good. Many users found that tough technical questions were met with shrugged shoulders and a request to read the manual again.

Despite having very technically successful products, these firms became sitting ducks once they had competitors focused on providing better service. In a very short period of time, a new breed of companies offering unlimited toll-free technical support dominated the PC software market, while many of the original firms quickly faded into the background. While competition continues to rage in this industry, with new players and new issues, this particular time period saw a near-total market shift from technology issues to service ones.

On a broader scale, a commitment to legendary service can define an entirely new market niche.

- Time was when most people ordered eyeglasses at the corner optical shop and waited weeks to get them. Then a company named LensCrafters built an optical chain based on a service concept – glasses in about an hour – rather than a product or price concept. They quickly tapped into a consumer need that propelled them to be leaders in the prescription eyewear industry.
- Legend has it that when FedEx chairman Fred Smith originally proposed the concept of a hub-and-spoke overnight delivery service in a paper for his college economics class, he received a "C" for it. Today, fueled by their People-Service-Profit philosophy, FedEx has defined the overnight delivery business to the point where customers often use its name as a verb – "We'll FedEx this package to you." In the process, it has grown to revenues of more than $14 billion per year, while being named as one of the 100 best companies to work for in America.
- From its roots in a college dormitory, Dell Computer became one of the world's largest retailers of personal computers by focusing on what they call "a bold strategy of direct customer contact." A pioneer in direct telephone sales of computers,

they later developed a web-based e-commerce model that grew from $1 million per day to over $30 million dollars per day in Internet-based sales in just two years. More importantly, their investments in infrastructure, distribution and award-winning service quality have now made Dell a household name for corporate and individual computer users worldwide.

Competition is relentless in every business, and these pressures will continue to drive trends such as the ones outlined here. The need to change, and sometimes change constantly, is perhaps the one constant in today's global marketplace. At the same time, by competing on legendary service as well as price and features, you have an opportunity to capture the one thing that cannot be easily taken away from you – the mindshare and loyalty of your customers. When you move from merely providing good service to creating a service-driven culture, you turn customers from purchasers into partners and advocates of your organization. These kinds of customers then become part of the business capital that insures your future success in a competitive market.

The seven steps: part of a greater whole

In this book, we have outlined seven key steps that are common to nearly all successful service-driven businesses. Each of them is essential, but more importantly, none of them can stand alone. They are part of a chain, from which any broken link can impact your reputation and market share. Truly legendary service is the product of a unified way of thinking that affects every aspect of your business.

Understanding this point is perhaps the most critical factor of all in your success as a service leader. This is why many businesses fail to provide good service despite external efforts such as training programs, customer surveys, focus groups, or mission and vision statements.

Once, I purchased a new computer that was dead on arrival once I got it home. When I called the computer manufacturer's toll-free service number, I was greeted by a very pleasant and articulate person who seemed more than willing to help. However, she couldn't answer even the most basic questions about how I could go about getting my computer fixed. At first, she didn't believe that I was entitled to on-site service, until I recited my warranty word-for-word to her. Then she had no idea how long it would take to get a service call, or how to arrange one, and suggested that I call back again the next morning.

The next morning, I was told that I had to contact yet another number, and the person at that number then told me sourly that it would be at least a three day wait for service. I then decided to make myself a happy customer by returning the computer to the store for a refund. Later that same day, I received a call from this manufacturer's "quality team", wanting me to rate various aspects of my satisfaction with this computer on a scale of 1 to 5. (Guess what ratings I gave?) The person taking my call gave no indication that any of my concerns would ever be addressed.

This was a classic case of a company who followed most of the steps in this book, but couldn't pull it all together and deliver quality service. They undoubtedly had things like customer skills training, toll-free 24-hour support, call quality monitoring, and customer satisfaction measurement. But a legendary service culture? To my ears as a customer, they seemed more like a bunch of people who weren't managed to care beyond the narrow boundaries of their own jobs. I doubt that anyone involved in the transaction even cared that I returned their product.

Against this backdrop, developing a legendary service culture represents nothing less than an opportunity for you and your business. It can become a key strategic weapon versus your competitors, and one that cannot be erased simply by lowering prices or running bigger advertisements. And many of the steps that will get you there cost you absolutely nothing. Building a service culture based on respect, productivity and teamwork – with your customers firmly in the driver's seat – starts with goals and action, not expenditures. When an organization makes legendary service quality its goal, there is often no limit on what the people in it can accomplish.

Legendary customer service: the best job in the world

When people and businesses make a real commitment to legendary customer service, the results can be nothing short of amazing – both for the bottom line, and the half of our waking lives or more that most of us spend at work. But perhaps more than any aspect of business, the drive to create service excellence goes far beyond profit and loss, or even individual careers. When it becomes a central part of who you are, it has the power to touch lives.

Albuquerque, New Mexico, quality consultant Dr. Milt Garrett describes the time that he decided to surprise his wife with a new car after a very special anniversary: her fifth year of surviving cancer. He ordered and paid for a white Saturn vehicle from his local dealership, where he explained the circumstances. When she was subsequently persuaded to stop by the dealership on a Saturday morning with her husband and son, there was a surprise there for all three of them. There on the white Saturn on the showroom floor was a professionally lettered sign that read:

"Congratulations, Jane.
This car is yours. Five years cancer free. Let's celebrate life.
From Milt, Billy [their sales consultant] and Team Saturn"

The sign included the signatures of every employee of the dealership, which had discreetly cleared all the customers from the showroom to allow them the privacy of a very special moment. Meanwhile, a growing crowd of people gathering outside the showroom applauded with emotion as his wife cried and fell into her husband's arms.

Experiences like these are the icing on the cake for what is perhaps the best job in the world: serving other people. Few endeavors teach you as many skills with so much value to your career and your entire life: interpersonal communications, negotiation, diplomacy and leadership. And if you look at the backgrounds of an increasing number of top managers and corporate leaders, you will see that people who are customer-focused have a direct path up the corporate ladder as well.

The quest to create truly legendary customer service represents one of the hidden keys to success for most organizations. Performed well, it represents a win-win situation for everyone involved: your customers, your organization, and yourself. My hope is that the seven steps in this book will lead you and your team members on a path that puts you in the company of today's service leaders. Good luck, and may your efforts be blessed with success.

Endnotes

1. Zemke, Ron, "The Service Revolution: Who Won?," *Management Review*, March 1997, v. 86 n. 3, p. 10.
2. Fierman, Jaclyn, "Americans Can't Get No Satisfaction," *Fortune*, Dec. 11, 1995.
3. Stewart, Thomas A., "A Satisfied Customer Isn't Enough," *Fortune*, July 21, 1997.
4. Rankin, Bob, "Amazon.com – Biggest Bookstore on the Web," Boardwatch Magazine, Feb. 1996.
5. Kirschenbaum, Howard and Valerie Land Henderson, editors. *The Carl Rogers Reader*. Houghton Mifflin, 1989.
6. Blitz, Marcia. *Donald Duck*. Harmony Press, 1979.
7. Schuller, Robert H. *Tough Times Never Last but Tough People Do!* Thomas Nelson, 1984.
8. *Lady and the Tramp* (movie). Walt Disney Productions, 1955.
9. Blanchard, Ken and Sheldon M. Bowles. *Raving Fans: A Revolutionary Approach to Customer Service*. William Morrow and Company, 1993.
10. Weinstein, Matt. *Managing to Have Fun*. Simon and Schuster, 1996.
11. *Conan the Barbarian* (movie). MCA/Universal Pictures, 1981.
12. Freiberg, Kevin and Jackie Freiburg. *Nuts! Southwest Airlines' Crazy Recipe for Business and Personal Success*. Bard Press, 1996.

13. Whiteley, Richard and Diane Hessan, *Customer-Centered Growth.* Addison-Wesley, 1996.

14. Ryan, Sean T. and Richard W. Tate, "1995's Top 10 Stupid Policies.," *Training Magazine*, Nov. 1995.

15. Ellis, Albert. *How to Stubbornly Refuse to Make Yourself Miserable About Anything – Yes, Anything!* Lyle Stuart, 1990.

16. Maltz, Maxwell. *Psycho-Cybernetics.* Prentice-Hall, 1960.

17. Jan Carlzon. *Moments of Truth.* HarperCollins, 1989.

18. Matson, Eric. "Two Billion Reasons Cisco's on the Net," *Fast Company*, Jan. 1997.

About the Author

Rich Gallagher is an experienced call center manager and corporate trainer who is widely published in the customer service and support profession.

As director of customer services for a West Coast engineering software firm, Rich helped drive its growth from a startup operation to a major company on the NASDAQ stock exchange. Currently he is president of Acuity Learning Group, a training and development firm based in upstate New York. *Delivering Legendary Customer Service* is his fourth book.

For more information on training programs related to this book, visit Acuity Learning Group at www.acuitylearninggroup.com. To learn more about Rich's books and publications, as well as additional tips to help your business succeed through excellent customer service, visit his web site at www.rsgallagher.com.

Printed in the United States
128551LV00003B/75/A